The Wonder
of Being Human
Our Brain and Our Mind

Sir John Eccles
Daniel N. Robinson

THE FREE PRESS
A Division of Macmillan, Inc.
NEW YORK

Collier Macmillan Publishers
LONDON

The Free Press
A Division of Macmillan, Inc.
866 Third Avenue, New York, N. Y. 10022

Collier Macmillan Canada, Inc.

Printed in the United States of America

printing number

1 2 3 4 5 6 7 8 9 10

Library of Congress Cataloging in Publication Data

Eccles, John C. (John Carew)
    The wonder of being human.

    1. Consciousness.   2. Intellect.   3. Ethics.
4. Mind and body.   5. Human biology.   I. Robinson,
Daniel N.   II. Title.
QP411.E28   1984   153   83-49044
ISBN 0-02-908860-7

The following illustrations are reprinted by permission:

Figures 3–1 and 9–3 (from Springer-Verlag, Heidelberg: J. C. Eccles, *Human Psyche,* 1980); 3–3, 3–4, 3–5, and 11–1 (from Springer-Verlag, Heidelberg: J. C. Eccles, *Human Mystery,* 1979); 8–2 (from Pergamon Press, Oxford: J. C. Eccles, "How the Self Acts on the Brain," *Psychoneuroendocrinology, 7* [4], February 1983); 3–2 (from Birkhäuser Verlag, Basel: J. C. Eccles, "Animal Consciousness and Human Self-consciousness," *Experientia, 38,* 1982); 9–1 (from J. Szentágothai); 9–2 (from H. H. Kornhüber); and 11–2 (from P. E. Roland).

For
Helena and Francine

Live unto the dignity of thy nature, and leave it not disputable at last, whether thou has been a man; or, since thou art a composition of man and beast, how thou hast predominantly passed thy days, to state the denomination. Unman not, therefore, thyself by a bestial transformation, nor realize old fables. Expose not thyself by four-footed manners unto monstrous draughts, and caricature representations. Think not after the old Pythagorean conceit, what beast thou mayst be after death. Be not under any brutal metempsychosis while thou livest and walkest about erectly under the scheme of man. In thine own circumference, as in that of the earth, let the rational horizon be larger than the sensible, and the circle of reason than of sense: let the divine part be upward, and the region of the beast below. . . . Desert not thy title to a divine particle and union with invisibles. Let true knowledge and virtue tell the lower world thou art part of the higher. . . .

Sir Thomas Browne (1605–1682)

Contents

v

Preface

Commentators too numerous to cite have discussed the steady erosion of life's "meaning" during these recent decades of material prosperity and unprecedented personal liberty. Much of this examination has been led by "self-help" specialists who habitually confuse mere coping with genuine personal growth. They have emphasized patterns of social adjustment promising little more than ephemeral pleasure and contentment, thus making their remedies just another version of the disease itself. There is in all of this a chilling neglect of what can only be called a *moral point of view*. Human life is regarded instead as a kind of machine requiring periodic maintainance; the dilemmas of life need "fixing."

What is the moral point of view, and how is it related to human happiness? These were questions raised by Socrates, and they have animated intellectual discourse for the better part of twenty-five centuries. Without being specific at this point, we may say that the moral point of view begins with man's awareness of the fact of his own transcendence; the recognition that human persons are different from and rise above those utterly material events comprised in the purely physical cosmos. Where this recognition has been blocked or defeated or depreciated, life has been less than fully human. In its absence there may be animal pleasures but not human happiness.

The social and scientific revolutions of the past two centuries have transformed our perspective on the most fundamental aspects of civilized life. What today's children take for granted about themselves and the natural world would have struck the most developed intelligences of the sixteenth or seventeenth century as simply incredible. It is, of course, a commonplace to note how discoveries in science and technology have changed our ways of doing things and thinking about them. What is often missed, however, is that the changes are recognized only half-consciously and that they invade regions of life and thought that have nothing to do with science itself. Even if a citizen has had special training in science, he is still conditioned in his daily perceptions by a pervasive *metaphysics* that imposes a definite character on the full range of cognitive, emotional, social, and aesthetic processes—the processes that are brought to bear on the serious matter of life. What begins as a discovery in science—or even no more than a scientific conjecture—is soon taken as a model or metaphor of some larger realm of human concern. In time, at the urging of the leaders of public opinion, the metaphor becomes installed as the reality, and the seasonless convictions of the ordinary person are thus put on official notice! Only years later, under reality's sobering lights, does it once again become clear that our ageless dilemmas have survived these once "new truths"; that the vexing problems of value have not surrendered to the thick and thickening book of fact; that the most recent revolutions of perspective have done little more than move us around that circle whose center is the human condition.

Scientific and humanistic studies are expressions and not the origins of the mind and its workings. As such, they must not be expected to reveal us more fully or more meaningfully than we know ourselves in that blunt introspective way. That scholarship illuminates some of the causes of which we are, in a manner of speaking, the "effects" may be true, but it is as these "effects" that we live each and all of our days. To alert the sufferer to the cause of his toothache is neither to dispel nor to address the irreducibly existential fact of pain, the private but indubitable pain that remains defiantly unaffected even though its causes are precisely catalogued.

Scientific and humanistic studies, as uniquely human affairs, are conducted by men and women whose personal needs and expectations are drawn from the general pool of human concerns. Accordingly, it is not unnatural for the scientist or humanist to go beyond the facts and theories that define his subject and to drag them into those utterly existential settings occupied by "mere citizens." That such a move may be logically impermissible or prudentially unsound is a possibility easily set aside by unfettered enthusiams. Once made, such a move gains momentum from the authority of scholarship, picking up disciples as it rolls down toward the public, and culminating its journey in the form of so massive and varied a body of fact, conjecture, and fancy as to be nearly impregnable. To the layman it is like some awful slot machine, which, for a penny, will tell him his fortune by showing him his *self,* his world. To the specialist it is a symbol of accomplishment and power, solid proof that his way is the right way, at least the best way. In the thrill of it all, it is difficult to perceive this thing as just one more cadaver upon which posterity will learn the anatomy of confusion.

But thoughtful persons do not have the luxury of declaring a pox on all these houses, retreating to the fatal comforts of know-nothingism. Indeed, the sudden revival of religious fundamentalism is in its own way but another symptom of the contemporary penchant for extremism. Men and women of all ages are now found espousing religious tenets that are nearly as mechanical as the psychiatric ones of a decade ago. Through an unbending orthodoxy these joyful believers would protect themselves from that unseemly world that is nonetheless their home. Their threats against the outsider make them laughable to the educated and ostensibly urbane citizens of this stridently secular world. When all of Christian history turns up no more than one Paul on the road to Damascus, credibility will not sustain the weight of numbers now claiming similar and daily visitations. Quite simply—if harshly—the judicious bystander is tempted to conclude that this recent fervor may prove to be at the expense of Christianity itself. It just won't do to bury science and thought in the hopes of thereby "saving the world." Saving it for what? Scientific curiosity and genius, like faith itself, cannot be excluded from any plausible account of the attributes of the developed human person. Ours and ours alone is the species of thinkers and believers, A war against thought is a war against self. The only defensible alternative is to embrace what is most sound in our science and scholarship as we attempt to penetrate more deeply into the wonders of human life. And it is this that we attempt in the following pages.

The plans for this book were made in the spring of 1981, when the first author was in residence at Georgetown University to give the inaugural series of Carroll Lectures. In long and frank discussions we became convinced of the need to expose any number of allegedly scientific theses that have depreciated the value of the human person and caused untold numbers to regard themselves and their lives as insignificant and pointless accidents of (material) nature. That these harmful and woefully defective lessons have been taught in the name of science made us additionally fearful that science itself would inherit the scorn of humanity.

Science is one of our greatest creations and surely one of the most dependable guides on the human adventure. It deserves nurturance and respect, for it is a worthy expression of human genius, rationality, and hope. It is, however, also subject to distortion and debasement. In the chapters of this book we will expose a number of *scientistic* fables or superstitions that have arisen from corruptions of genuine science. In the process we will be unembarrassed in our celebrations of the wonders of human nature, but we would not want our appraisals mistaken for that uncritical humanism that has now become epidemic. Our appeal is to reason and moral sensibility, not to the reader's vanities. In establishing the uniqueness and preciousness of the human person, we would hope that readers would come to shun all venal purposes on which too many of today's lives are wasted.

Like any serious endeavor of multiple authorship, the present work may be marred by abrupt transitions in tone and content. To help readers fix the blame, we note here that Chapters 2, 3, 6, 9, and 11 are chiefly the responsibility of J. C. E. and are based on his Carroll Lectures at Georgetown. Chapters 1, 4, 5, 7, and 10 are chiefly the responsibility of D.N.R., and Chapters 8 and 12 were written jointly. In all cases each of us benefited from the other's criticisms and suggestions.

After each chapter there follows a list of publications for consultation. The references of the authors contain extensive bibliographies and could themselves be consulted for more elaborate treatments of the ideas presented in the various chapters of this book; J.C.E. has indicated the appropriate chapters to refer to in his publications. Some citations give reference to ideas differing from those expressed in this book.

Complete agreement between authors is not to be expected when issues of such complexity and subtlety are addressed. We are nonetheless satisfied that the major propositions and assessments developed in the book faithfully reflect our shared judgments.

1

Nature and Human Nature

It takes no deep philosophical insight to recognize the connection between what a person does and what a person thinks he is, between what others expect of us and what they think of us. So close is this connection that much of social and political history can be understood in just these terms. Whether one takes human beings to be "children of God," "tools of production," "matter in motion," or "a species of primate" has consequences. As long as such notions remain within the private sanctuaries of academic quibbling, their consequences are largely only literary. But when any of them wanders beyond the high gates of scholarship and comes to command the loyalties of significant numbers of citizens, the effects on government, culture, and daily life can be and have been dramatic.

Our own age is one in which ideas move with unprecedented speed. Whole clouds of speculation now routinely settle over the general public before scholars ever have time to test the vapors for their effects on the ecology of thought. A relatively unpopular and unsuccessful television program can claim twenty million viewers, many of them holding positions of power and responsibility. In a single year the average citizen is exposed to as many hours of such entertain-

1

ment, ideology, information, and persuasion as may have been contained in the entire history of his formal education. And when we add to the formidable influences of television the accumulated effects of radio, motion pictures, newspapers and "bestsellers," we discover how it is that the most informed population in the history of the human race is also one of the most confused, despairing, and unsettled. The problem is not that the modern citizen "knows too much" but that there has been insufficient preparation for weighing, testing, and judging the larger implications of what is known.

Democracy's most fervent defenders have always been fearful of the *tyranny of the majority*. But until quite recently such fears have been relieved by the fact that majorities have been difficult to form and to maintain. This once durable protection has been eroded by the technology of persuasion. Increasingly, therefore, we discover the quick establishment of "official" views on all sorts of issues that have divided scholars for centuries. In any mass culture it is to be expected that mere opinion will enjoy greater authority than close analysis. This is a more or less benign fact as long as opinions vary widely while careful analyses (predictably) lead to a consensus among the few who "live to think." When opinion becomes homogenized, however, it takes on its tyrannical pretensions. Quickly lost sight of is the fact that mere opinion remains *opinion* no matter how many share it. Rather, and insensibly, the public comes to conclude that a widespread belief expresses a veritable law of nature.

Today we have any number of such widespread or at least widely spreading beliefs; beliefs that give color and form to what later historians will take to be the "folk psychology," "folk morality," and "folk science" of our epoch. These are the beliefs that have come to control what we think of ourselves and others; what we have come to expect of ourselves and others; what we judge to be the nature, the purpose, and the possibilities of our lives. What we hope to convey in the following pages is the fact that much that goes into these now very popular views is either provably false or utterly speculative; and further, that a more realistic, scientific, and coherent appraisal of human *persons* leaves room for opportunities that the modern citizen has all but abandoned.

Surely one of the most durable issues in the history of thought has to do with whether human nature is merely one aspect of nature or whether it is something that stands apart from the natural order. Philosophers of nearly every religious persuasion have been found on each side of the issue, which would seem to be proof enough that it is not simply a question of belief or conviction. Nor is it a purely abstract question. The actions and goals of people are very much influenced by the sort of being they think they are. Indeed, to a striking degree the very character of laws, governments, educational institutions, and international relations has depended historically on fundamental notions about the nature of human nature. One need only consider such phrases as "the divine right of kings" or "the African is a slave by nature" or "Pharaoh is the living god" to recall how entire epochs have been colored and shaped by eccentric theories about ourselves and others.

But every epoch is generally far more uncritical about its own perspective than about those embraced by an earlier age. The citizen of today's Western democracies can only smile when thinking of those innocent ancestors who really believed that God had specifically chosen the reigning monarch and had bestowed special rights on him; or those more remote ancestors who stocked pharaoh's crypt with all he would need on the long journey to immortal glory. The smile becomes one of embarrassment as we recall that widely held conviction of the eighteenth and nineteenth centuries by which entire races of man were taken to be just slightly higher than beasts of burden—and not on the same continuum with the civilized European!

We take such notions now to be no more than the ruling fictions of the past; preposterous superstitions adopted by the ignorant and exploited by the clever; the merely habitual fancies of the unlit mind. History, however, though it *waits* for us, does not *end* with us. We and our assortment of theories and prejudices will serve as subjects for the future historians. They will wonder, no doubt, about the easy confidence we display in all sorts of fashionable ideas and, after assessing them, will place our age back among the specimens of wisdom and folly.

We will all be dead and gone, of course, when these judgments are made, but this is no reason not to leave a good impression. If only for this reason—and there are far more compelling reasons—we must periodically take stock of our most common conceptions and be prepared to acknowledge that many of them come under the heading of rank ideology, a superstition. Historical survey reveals that each age has had its cherished superstitions. A new age dawns with their identification and rejection. A new crop of superstitions waits in the wings. All of our superstitions will be rebuked by a more discerning posterity, but some of them are mischievous in our own time and should be uprooted even if there were to be no future to look back on us.

Which conceptions are these? They are numerous but not easy

to name. They all contain an element of truth but are fatally defective in the radical form in which they appear today. They are often alleged to be "scientific," but their contact with genuine science is never more than tangential and usually entirely specious. They arise from the rich and ripe traditions of philosophy but have now been transformed into little more than a kind of propaganda. They tend to be defended by most of "the right people," who, in an age such as ours, however, are scarcely more informed than those they would presume to lead.

Before setting forth these conceptions—today's official "isms" —a word of caution is in order. It is not our view that the majority of people consciously adopt any or all of them or that a quiet conspiracy is laboring to foist them on the unsuspecting. In referring to these conceptions of human nature as "isms" we mean to identify them only as a part of a contemporary folk philosophy, not as the formal propositions of a developed *school* of thought. For tens of centuries the average observer took for granted that the earth is stationary and that the sun revolves around it. We can say that this observer was not a disciple of *Copernicanism* without suggesting that he consciously and critically associated himself with any formal and competing *ism*. We can, that is, classify his conceptions as *Ptolemaic,* knowing all the while that he never heard of Ptolemy. So too with the *isms* we are now to discuss. They stand at the very core of modern thought and action, though they are seldom subjected to public scrutiny or to the average citizen's own private analysis.

1. *Scientism.* Where Scripture was once that court of last recourse in which every claimed truth had to plead its case, science is now taken to be the ultimate arbiter. It is difficult today to discover any significant proposal for government, social life, interpersonal relations, education, morality, or personal happiness that is not defended in "scientific" terms or criticized for being "unscientific." There is now a near-synonymy between "true" and "scientific" and a general conviction that what is not "scientific" cannot be true. Thus does the layman turn to the "behavioral sciences" and the "social sciences" for direction in matters of daily life the way he might turn to physics and chemistry for direction in his understanding of brute nature. As he understands things, the realm of thought is filled by only two kinds of entities, scientific *truth* and utterly subjective *opinion*. There can, therefore, be no valid basis for opposing anything that science has not legislated against or for defending what science has not established.

2. *Relativism.* Once the layman has convinced himself that there are only the *facts* of science and the *fancy* of opinion, it is a short step to the conclusion that even the most fundamental principles of morality and justice are largely *relative* to a certain point of view. Accordingly "our morality" is but one of a vast number of possible moralities, the choice of any of them depending on who is in power. For a society to be free, therefore, necessarily implies that it will be "pluralistic," for the simple reason that opinions vary. Since there is no *scientifically* validated morality, anything goes!

3. *Materialism.* We use "materialism" in its formal philosophical sense and not as a description of the buying habits of the middle class. Science has turned up nothing more than *matter* in its investigations of the universe. Human life, too, therefore can be only and exhaustively *material.* As a result of our biological organization, we are machines of a certain type, designed to avoid damage and to approach whatever enhances survival. Our most basic impulses are grounded in the experiences of pleasure and pain. Such personal or institutional arrangements as we might form or be drawn into are to be understood solely in terms of these impulses. We may speak in the elevated language of reason and ethics, but even our most rational and principled creations—law, foreign policy, a respect for the "rights" of others—are simply expressions of a fundamentally selfish core of biologically determined emotions. This has been emphatically expressed by E. G. Wilson in his book *On Human Nature.*

4. *Evolutionism.* Granting 1, 2, and 3 above, it follows that the most coherent account of the origin and essential nature of human nature is the one developed by Charles Darwin and refined by his disciples. The facts standing in support of the "theory" of evolution are so numerous and compelling that it is no longer necessary to think of the Darwinian account as "theory" at all. Except for the self-deceptions of religion, all reasonable persons would agree that humanity is just another form of biological organization created out of the long seasons of fierce competition and the short seasons of genetic mutation. We hold no special place in the scheme of things, for in the scheme of things there are only *things*—purely material things whose complexity is fully explained by the laws of evolutionary science.

5. *Environmentalism.* The struggle for survival can be won only by animals able to conform their behavior to the demands of the environment. Among the simpler forms of life this ability comes by way of instinct. The more advanced forms, such as mammals, are able to adapt by benefiting from past experience. That is, they can learn and

remember. Human beings are especially effective at this mode of adaptation, a mode shaped over eons in the history of the species and during every waking moment in the life of the individual. What one does, therefore, or comes to want or believe or strive for is just what the environment has "planted" in him. Through the management of rewards and punishments, society is able to produce the sorts of citizens it desires. Mistakes are made, and so criminality and insanity will occur and will add to the number of deviants resulting from biological accidents. By and large, however, with the accidents of biology set aside, the given person is a creation of the environment; an environment that has exploited the natural instinct to survive in such a way as to secure compliance. And we can be sure of all this because it has been established by the "behavioral sciences"!

It is our view that these five truisms of today's folk philosophy have much to do with the dissatisfaction and aimlessness infecting modern life and that they deny the modern citizen the pleasure and happiness of the human adventure. It is our judgment, as will become clear in the following pages, that each of these truisms is incoherent, implausible, or provably false when subjeced to close examination.

What we hope to accomplish in the following chapters is an instructive though surely not exhaustive review of the concepts germane to personhood as science now possesses them and a defensible collection of inferences from these concepts. For the inferences to be weighed by the reader, it is necessary to provide a working scientific vocabulary, which we try to make as painless as possible. It is also necessary for the reader to be acquainted with influential theories, both current and traditional, that continue to direct scientific energies and popular enthusiasms. In the process we hope to carve away from *personhood* any number of attributes wrongly grafted onto it and, by the book's end, to present a more faithful rendering of the special beings we are.

We begin, then, at the beginning, with the origins of life, of man, and of mind on Planet Earth.

Suggested Readings

Bock, K. E. *Human nature and history.* New York: Columbia University Press, 1980.

ROBINSON, D. N. *Systems of modern psychology: A critical sketch.* New York: Columbia University Press, 1979.

SKINNER, B. F. *Beyond freedom and dignity.* New York: Knopf, 1971.

WILSON, E. O. *On human nature.* Cambridge, Mass.: Harvard University Press, 1978.

2

The Origins of Life, Mind, and Man

Life

THE PREBIOTIC WORLD

Let us imagine a traveler from outer space, three and a half billion years ago, who, after visiting many celestial objects, came upon Planet Earth. After the stony wastelands of Mars and the Moon it would be enthused by the tremendous oceans with their ever varied coastlines, the great ice fields of the polar areas and of the mountains, the terrible beauty of the multitudinous volcanoes, the entrancing beauty of the sky and clouds with the play of sunlight on them, and the gorgeous colors of the sunrises and sunsets. Such entrancing beauty and wonder were exhibited by Planet Earth some hundreds of millions of years after its cooling from the original molten state, with its rocks solidified into the thin stony crust it still has and with its water vapor condensed to make the oceans.

Yet the greatest wonder was still to come to this prebiotic world. This hitherto lifeless planet was to become "infected" by life in a way that still defeats our imagination and our understanding. Some of the organic chemical molecules that are essential for the creation of the earliest forms of life exist in interstellar space and so could descend to Planet Earth. However, more important we think is the production of these chemicals from the gases of the prebiotic atmosphere by the electric discharges of lightning, by cosmic rays, and by ultraviolet radiation, as has been demonstrated by Miller, Calvin, Orgel, and others. So for hundreds of millions of years there would have been the accumulation of large quantities of organic molecules essential for life: amino acids, purine and pyrimidine bases, sugars, and so on. Concentration of these molecules could occur in shallow pools by evaporation to give what is poetically described as a dilute soup! Optimistically we can now think we have the right medium for culturing the earliest living forms, the *eobacteria,* which can be recognized as fossils in the most ancient rocks (the cherts) and can be dated at 3,500 million years ago. The culture medium may be right, but the creation of the most primitive life is much the greater wonder.

THE CREATION OF LIFE

All life is based on two classes of complex organic molecules, nucleic acids and proteins. Nucleic acids are the essential constituents of the double helix, deoxyribonucleic acid (DNA), which carries in code the instructions for building deoxyribonucleic acids and proteins, some of the proteins being the enzymes necessary for using the codes in the building operations. Given that in the primordial soup pools there are assembled the raw materials—amino acids, purine and pyrimidine bases, sugars and phosphates—for building proteins and nucleic acids, the conundrum is that proteins (enzymes) cannot be built without enzymes. It is like the hen and the egg. The resolution of this conundrum is exercising great chemists (Manfred Eigen and his associates), who are imaginatively constructing model systems of hypercyclic chemical operations that could resolve the initial enigmas. But even when that is accomplished, it is only the first step in accounting for the origin of the simplest living organism that could maintain its integrity as a unit, utilize energy, grow, and reproduce so that it can duplicate itself with the accuracy necessary for an indefinitely prolonged multiplication sequence. We are far from that level of understanding; yet life did begin on this planet 3,500 million years ago, and

it did survive and flourish and diversify despite the countless vicissi-
tudes in the thousands of millions of years since that time. It is of great
interest to note that all living forms to this day—microorganisms,
plants, and animals—share the same essential constituents in their
genetic material and the same twenty amino acids in their proteins.
This argues for a uniquely single origin of life from which all the immense diversity has stemmed and for the extreme improbability of
this origin. Apparently this transcendent happening was a unique oc-
casion.

Meanwhile we have to await the unfolding of the story of the origin of life. We can anticipate that the essential manner of origin will
be identified and modeled, and that more and more of the stages will
be revealed. Recently Francis Crick and Leslie Orgel have resur-
rected the hypothesis that Planet Earth was ''seeded'' by primitive
living organisms from ''elsewhere'' and that life was not a local product! This most unhelpful suggestion merely relegates the mystery of
origin to another site. It has an obscurantist character and solves
nothing.

THE DEVELOPMENT OF LIFE

Let us now go on from what is known. Fossils of the earliest known organisms show that they resemble bacteria and are called *eobacteria*.
Since the primitive atmosphere had almost no oxygen, the eobacteria
had to derive their energy from the organic materials of the ''soup,''
and they had the disability that their precious genetic material, DNA,
was just lying in loose coils among the various organelles of the cell's
interior, as is the case with all bacteria and all other *prokaryotes,* as they
are called, even to this day. It is generally believed that the eobacteria
ran into difficulties with depletion of their food, which had been built
by prebiotic chemistry and concentrated in the primitive ''soup.''
Fortunately, after some hundreds of millions of years mutations resulted in the development of living organisms with alternative energy
sources. The most notable is the use of pigments for photosynthetic
metabolism, using sunlight, as is done by the blue-green algae by
means of the green pigment chlorophyll. Bacteria also developed
other pigments for photosynthesis. The blue-green algae came to
dominate the shallow waters, forming immense structures whose fossil remains, *stromatolites,* are so striking today. Under the influence of
sunlight the chlorophyll of these algae converts carbon dioxide and
water into oxygen and sugar. So over some billions of years the oxy-

gen of the earth's atmosphere was created from the primitive atmosphere that contained negligible levels of oxygen and high levels of carbon dioxide from the "outgassing" of volcanoes.

In the fossil record the first appearing multicellular organisms are jellyfish and worms, some 700 million years ago. Of the 2 to 3 billion years preceding that, all we can say is that the oxygen of the atmosphere was built up to about one-half of its present level and that there was an improvement in the genetic arrangement of organisms (called *eukaryotes*) with the precious genetic code of the DNA collected into nuclei central to the cells for its protection and for its participation in the process of reproduction, presumably with the reduction of copying errors. If we consider the time scale of the existence of living organisms, what seems beyond imagining is the enormous duration of the simplest prokaryotic phase for some 1,600 million years before the rearrangement of the genetic material in the eukaryotes. We can be concerned at this terribly slow rate of progress, especially when we realize that this was the progress that eventually led to our appearance on the stage of the cosmic drama!

With the coming of multicellular organisms some 700 million years ago cell differentiation for diverse functions was instituted, and with that the fantastic innovative powers of biological evolution were revealed. Its occurrence could never have been predicted after almost 3 billion years of unicellular life. The story of life can now be diagrammed in the branching trees for the animals on the one hand and for the plants on the other, with the phyla branching to orders, to families, to genera, to species. There are hundreds of thousands and, in the order of *insecta* alone, millions of species. If we could be transported back in time to observe on an enormously accelerated time scale the story of multicellular organisms, from 700 million years ago to the present time, we could be witnessing the wonderful pageant of creation. We can even now experience in our imagination the evolutionary procession with creatures of utmost diversity bravely flourishing, surviving and dying out. For example, the fossil record shows, from 500 million years ago, the flourishing of the arthropod *Trilobite*, with its exquisite eyes, but Trilobites were extinct by 200 million years ago. The great dinosaurs dominated the earth from 225 million years ago but were extinct by 65 million years ago. Thereafter our mammalian ancestors came to dominate the scene after a long period of bare survival from 200 million years ago. About 70 million years ago the primitive mammals diversified enormously, and the *age of the mammals* begins at 65 million years ago.

Our remote primate forebears, the prosimians, appeared as early as 70 million years ago, but the primate fossil record is very incomplete, so the details of the hominid origin are still debatable. Common ancestors of apes and hominids have been identified as *Aegyptopithecus, Dryopithecus,* and *Ramapithecus,* the last differentiating into a prehominid. But there is no fossil record of it after 8 million years ago, and the first hominids (*Australopithecus*) cannot be identified before 5 million years ago. A great improvement in the fossil record is urgently needed. We necessarily are biased observers of the pageant of evolution and will be concentrating on the evolutionary line that eventually led to our immediate ancestors, *Homo sapiens,* some 200,000 years ago.

THE DARWINIAN THEORY OF EVOLUTION

The Darwinian theory must rank as one of the grandest scientific achievements and has immense explanatory power. There is no alternative theory. However, it has to be recognized that, with the growth of knowledge of the fossil record and of molecular biology, the theory of biological evolution will be much modified. There is the danger of its being prematurely hardened into a dogma when its explanatory power is still deficient and it is almost untested, as discussed in Chapter 5.

In its essential form there are two components of the theory. First there are the *mutations* of the genetic material, the genes based on *deoxyribonucleic acid* (*DNA*). Mutations are small changes in the molecular structure of DNA. They arise purely by chance, for example as a consequence of some damaging chemical or radiation, and are not determined even to the smallest extent by any need conducive to an improved survival power of the organism. Second, there is *natural selection,* which ensures preservation of those gene combinations most conducive to survival. Animals with unfavorable gene combinations are eliminated in competition with those more favorably endowed. In every single generation there is selection by the survival test of mutations arising by chance.

Later we shall see that the explanatory power of this evolutionary theory is deficient in important respects. Meanwhile it should be pointed out that this official theory of biological evolution precludes any *guidance* of evolutionary development by long-range goals, as is proposed for example by the theory of *Finalism* that is associated with Teilhard de Chardin. On the contrary, the official theory is essentially opportunistic, natural selection being concerned only with the survival and propagation of a particular generation, and then again (opportunistically) for the next, and so on. It is the dogma that, by an initial process of pure chance (the gene mutations), there can be wrought by natural selection all of the marvelous structural and functional features of living organisms with their amazing adaptiveness and inventiveness. The crux of the matter is that it is *our* origin that is prescribed in the dogma. Are we to find it acceptable that our very existence as self-conscious beings is to be incorporated in the stark dogma of chance and necessity as spelled out by Jacques Monod? Later there will be a searching exploration of this question of origins. We shall be considering the origin of mind and self-conscious mind later in this chapter, and Chapter 8 will contain a consideration of hominid evolution.

Mind: Animal Consciousness

INTRODUCTION

In recent years biologists and psychologists have been emerging from the long, dark night of behaviorism, where it was regarded as scientifically inadmissable to raise questions concerning the consciousness of animals. Fortunately this darkness has been dispelled by the writings of, for example, Thorpe, Lorenz, and Griffin.

We can speak of an animal as conscious when it is moved apparently by feelings and moods and when it is capable of assessing its present situation in the light of past experience and so is able to arrive at an appropriate course of action that is more than a stereotyped instinctive response. In this way it can exhibit an original behavior pattern that can be learned and that also includes a wealth of emotional reactions. A good example is the ape in a closed room with a movable box in one corner and a bunch of bananas in the other, suspended too high to reach. After long cogitation the ape moves the box under the bananas and succeeds. A quite different demonstration of conscious experiences is given by the spontaneous play of mammals, particularly of the young.

THE EVOLUTION OF CONSCIOUSNESS

The evolutionary story looks clear enough until we ask questions: How in the evolutionary process did mind or animal consciousness come into existence in a hitherto mindless world? How early in the evolutionary development of animals did they come to experience mental events, gleams of mental experiences first appearing out of the hitherto all-pervasive darkness? Such mental events must be related to the ongoing neural events of the brain, but how do they improve the performance of the brain and so become valuable for evolutionary survival? Finally, what ontological status can we ascribe to mental events that have appeared in a world that heretofore could be considered monistically as a material world—the world of matter and energy?

Clearly we are in deep trouble. When such troubles arise in the history of thought, it is usual to adopt some belief that "saves" the day. For example, the denial of the reality of mental events, as in radical materialism, is an easy cop-out. It must be an embarrassing belief to acknowledge publicly when it is recognized as negating even one's own conscious belief and experiences! Radical materialism should have a prominent place in the history of human silliness. The alternative is to espouse panpsychism (Teilhard de Chardin, Rensch, Birch). All types of panpsychists evade the problems by proposing that there is a protoconsciousness in all matter, even in elementary particles! According to panpsychism the evolutionary development of brain is associated merely with an amplification and refinement of what was already there as a property of all matter. It merely is exhibited more effectively in the complex organizations of the brains of higher animals. Thus there is an easy solution to the problem of the emergence of mind in association with enhanced brain performance. We do not regard this as an acceptable solution. It is a too easy evasion of the problem by proposing a radical transformation of physics, as will be discussed below.

If as neuropsychologists we study the behavior of simple organisms, even honey bees, we can plausibly account for even the most complex behavior by the concept of inherited instinct with a superimposed learning. The instinctual performance of an animal is based on the ontogenetic building of its nervous system and related structures by means of the coded genetic instructions. And learning can be the increased effectiveness of synapses following usage (Chapter 9). Thus we can stay entirely within the materialistic order. By far the most studied behavior of animals below birds and mammals is that of the honey bee, but we do not accept Griffin's mentalistic assumptions for the honey bee on the grounds of dance patterns that display an elaborated coded symbolism with patterns in space and time. There is no reason to assume that the bees *know* what they do.

Even at the level of the amphibian it is possible to account for the very effective fly-catching of frogs in simple terms of visual recognition (bug detectors) and reactions thereto. Konrad Lorenz from his immense experience with birds describes behavior patterns indicating mental states. William Thorpe's experiments on number recognition by birds lead him to conclude: "We have extremely strong evidence that animals can perform the mental abstraction of the quality of number which in human children can only be accomplished by conscious cerebration."

It would seem that the range of our problem of mental phylogenesis can be reduced to birds and mammals. The simplest strategy would be that we study consciousness in performance of the highest nonhuman animals, the anthropoid apes, before considering the more marginal cases of the lower families of mammals and the birds.

Studies on chimpanzees in the wild reveal a rather limited performance: a very marginal use of "tools" without any conservation; an inability to use stones or sticks in effective combat; a restriction of interest to pragmatic considerations, food, social dominance, and sexual activity; and aggressiveness with at most a limited altruism in food sharing. Yet, when trained from babyhood, it has been possible to teach a considerable sign language (for example 130 signs for Gardner's "Washoe") that is skillfully used for pragmatic requests—for food, for tactile pleasure, for play, for expression of emotions, moods, and feeling tones, all at a level of a human child of a year and a half to two years, as described in Chapter 8. It can hardly be doubted that they have experiences of the same general nature as what we term conscious. Yet they fail to develop linguistically as does a human child using sign language, because they use language almost entirely pragmatically. There is little or no attempt to ask questions about the surrounding world in the effort to understand it (the mathetic use of language) as is done by a two- to three-year-old child with its torrent of questions. What is perplexing is the rudimentary character of the mental performance of an anthropoid ape when considered relative to its rather large brain of a distinctively human character.

There can be no doubt about the mental experiences of domesticated animals, the dog, cat, and horse. The play of young animals is a convincing criterion of consciousness, as also are curiosity and the display of emotions, in particular the evidence of devoted attachment. Still, we must be cautious about identifying these assumed mental states of animals with those humanly experienced. As described in Chapter 8, we lack symbolic communication with animals at the subtle level possible between human persons.

We can now ask: What advantage was given by this emergence of mental experiences associated with cerebral actions? For example, William James suggested that mind was a property acquired by a brain that had grown too complex to control itself. There have been suggestions that consciousness is valuable in that it gives some global experience to the animal. We would like to develop this idea further with respect of visual experience.

In the last two decades there has been an immense amount of scientific study on the processing of visual information in the brains of cats and monkeys. In this sequential processing there is a progressive abstraction from the features·of the original picture that existed as an image on the retina. At no stage in the nervous processing can neurones be found that would be instrumental in an eventual neural reconstruction of the picture, each carrying within itself uniquely some particular picture—the mythical "grandmother cells" that tell you when your grandmother is being seen! Yet we perceive the picture. The immense diversity of the patterned activity of neurones carries the coded information that could be used for reconstruction of the picture, but such a global operation apparently cannot be done by the mechanism of the cerebral cortex. It is, however, accomplished in the conscious visual experience that in a magical manner appears when we open our eyes and that changes from moment to moment in apparent synchrony with the visual inputs. The complex processing operations of the neural mechanism of the visual cortex and beyond carry the coded information that appears in the spatiotemporal patterns of the neuronal activity in the cerebral cortex. It can be postulated that in evolution the emergence of conscious mental experiences matched the evolution of the visual processing mechanism and its use in guiding the behavior of the animal.

Simpler visual inputs guiding simpler animal behavior may not require integration into a global visual picture. For example, as referred to above, the visual system of the frog may function without any integrative operation. But, with the greatly improved visual systems of the higher animals, birds and mammals, an integrated picture would be of great advantage in natural selection. Moreover this integration could include other sensory inputs—sound, smell, and tactile—thus giving some unified mental experience such as we enjoy.

Thus the hypothesis is developed that the emergence of mental experiences can be understood as providing for integration of the wide diversity of inputs into the brains of highly developed animals.

Animals with simpler nervous systems and more limited sensory inputs and behavioral outputs have no such requirement of integration beyond what can be given by the central nervous system. It is recognized that this hypothesis provides no explanation of the mysterious evolutionary emergence of mental experiences in a world hitherto purely physical in its attributes. It merely suggests how this emergence would give evolutionary advantage.

THE ENIGMA OF THE EVOLUTIONARY ORIGIN OF
CONSCIOUSNESS

It will be realized that the modern Darwinian theory of evolution is defective in that it does not even recognize the extraordinary problem presented by living organisms' acquiring mental experiences of a nonmaterial kind that are in another world from the world of matter-energy, which heretofore was globally comprehensive. The Cartesian solution is no longer acceptable, namely that human beings have conscious experiences that are attributable to the Divine creation of souls, and that higher animals are merely machine-like automata devoid of mental experiences. Likewise, as stated above, the panpsychist evasion of the problem is not acceptable.

There is also the problem of how mental experiences are derived from the neural mechanisms of the brain and how they feed back to bring about the appropriate reactions of the animal. These problems will be discussed in Chapter 3 in relation to human self-consciousness.

It is disturbing that evolutionists have largely ignored the tremendous enigma presented to their materialistic theory by the emergence of mentality in the animal evolution. For example there is no reference to the evolution of mentality in Mayr's classic book *Animal Species and Evolution,* in Monod's *Chance and Necessity* or in Wilson's *Sociobiology: The New Synthesis.* The explanation presumably is that, as is well documented by Griffin in his book *The Question of Animal Awareness,* the climate of opinion of biologists has been governed by the dogmas of the behaviorists. But ''animal awareness'' at least for the higher animals must now be accepted, and with that comes the challenge to the evolutionists. We have reached the stage where ignoring the problem will not cause it to go away. Darwin naively asked, ''Why is thought being a secretion of the brain, more wonderful than gravity, a property of matter?'' So he set the tone for all subsequent evolutionists to ignore the problem of the emergence of consciousness in the evolution of animals, including human beings. It was regarded simply as a derivation of cerebral development. By contrast Popper states: ''The emergence of consciousness in the animal kingdom is perhaps as great a mystery as the origin of life itself. Nevertheless, one has to assume, despite the impenetrable difficulty, that it is a product of evolution, of natural selection.''

We believe that the emergence of consciousness is a skeleton in the closet of orthodox evolutionism. At the same time it is recognized that, although the global concept formulated above allows for the development of animal consciousness by natural selection, it provides no explanation of this emergence. It remains just as enigmatic as it is to an orthodox evolutionist as long as it is regarded as an exclusively natural process in an exclusively materialist world. In the Epilogue of his first Gifford Lecture, ''The Human Mystery,'' Eccles concluded with a statement that is relevant to emergence:

> In the context of Natural Theology, I believe that there is a Divine Providence operating over and above the materialist happenings of biological evolution . . . we must not dogmatically assert that biological evolution in its present form is the ultimate truth. Rather we should believe it is the main story and that in some mysterious way there is guidance in the evolutionary chain of contingency.

America in particular has witnessed what is called the ''Creationist Revival,'' with even an Institute for Creation Research. The strategy has been to expose inadequacies in the theory of biological evolution and then to parade the creationist doctrine based on a literal interpretation of Genesis. They have quoted from Gould and Eldridge as questioning Darwinian thought. No doubt they will be utilizing our critical statements to the same effect. The defense against this anachronistic movement is to present the theory of biological evolution as a scientific hypothesis of immense explanatory power, there being absolutely no alternative in its essential features, but at the same time to recognize its inadequacies and to welcome informed criticism and the suggested modifications arising therefrom. The atmosphere should be that of flexible dialogue in the proper scientific manner and not the intransigent defense of a dogma.

Actually the evolutionary situation is much more open than it was in the 1930s and 1940s, in the era of the ''Modern Synthesis.'' It should be noted that Alfred Wallace, the co-discoverer with Charles Darwin of the principle of natural selection, repeatedly insisted that a purely materialistic explanation of biological evolution failed to account for the spiritual nature of man, ''and for this origin we can only find a cause in the unseen universe of spirit.''

The Beginning of Human Life

FETAL LIFE

The origin of each of us has been as a fertilized ovum or *zygote* that begins to subdivide in a few hours, becoming an assemblage of 2, 4, 8, 16 . . . cells by successive divisions. Rarely, the cells of the first division separate to make paired organisms that grow to be identical twins. Having the same genetic constitution, the two organisms are amazingly similar, for they are guided as developing human beings by identical genetic instructions. With extreme rarity there even may be separation at the stage of one further division. There are in Milano, Italy, *identical triplets,* three attractive and vivacious young women, all medical students. They regard their similarity as a joyous feature, each recognizing her individuality in the shared life of enriched experiences.

The precise vegetative or nutritional circumstances of the human being developing from the zygote are not absolutely crucial to its development as a fetus and then a baby. But it is vulnerable at certain stages to maternal infections, such as rubella and syphilis, and also to intoxication by drugs, thalidomide being a tragic example.

In normal circumstances the zygote migrates for some days before becoming implanted in the wall of the uterus, the endometrium being specially prepared for its reception by the phase of the menstrual cycle. When the fertilization of the ovum by a spermatozoon is carried out artificially, ''in a test tube,'' the developing *morula* has to be inserted into the uterus of the mother during the receptive phase. Otherwise it is unable to implant itself. Thereafter its intrauterine life normally progresses to term. Many normal babies have now been produced by this ethical procedure. It is even conceivable that techniques will be discovered for growing a human morula right up through its fetal stages and to babyhood by provision of a *correct* material environment, in the manner of Aldous Huxley's *Brave New World.* But extreme safeguards would have to be taken, else the baby would suffer damage from the inadequacies of the artificial environment. One hopes that it will be a rarely, if ever, justified enterprise. Implantation of the morula into a foster mother's uterus will be forever the greatly preferred alternative, and this is now a fairly common ethical procedure.

In the normal course of pregnancy the form of the fetus develops early, with a beating heart at three to four weeks. It is recognizably human at about fourteen weeks, though minute in size. Soon it is making its presence felt by movements. A systematic study of fetal movements in two thousand pregnancies, has used ultrasonic techniques. The first movements occur at six to eight weeks in the minute fetus, long before the mother feels them. By twenty weeks the fetus is learning the sounds generated in the mother's body, notably the heartbeat and the alimentary and respiratory movements. More surprisingly, it is learning the mother's voice! A microphone placed in the vagina picks up the maternal sounds approximately as these are heard by the fetus. It is instructive to compare the mother's speech in the air with that picked up vaginally, as has been done by Dr. Marie-Claire Busnel. Vowel sounds are less distorted than consonants, and singing is well heard. That the fetus is recognizing these sounds is established by its movements and by the altered heart rate in response to sudden changes in the mother's voice. The fetus also responds to mechanical stimuli. Pain is a very primitive sensation and should be felt by the fetus in response to some damaging stimulus, but mercifully there seems to have been no systematic investigation. One can only suspect that the induction of abortion causes the fetus severe pain before its death.

FETUS TO BABY

It is important to recognize that in brain development and functioning there is a *continuum* throughout fetal life and babyhood. Birth as such is but an unimportant incident along this continuum—a change in the mode of respiratory and nutritive mechanisms. In one way or the other the essential supply of oxygen, with the appropriate nutrients, is provided by the blood supply to the brain, which is large and rapidly growing. The newborn baby also has to accommodate itself to the change from weightless floating to gravitational force, to the experiences of vision, and to the new burden of temperature regulation. The dull monotony of the taste and smell of amniotic fluid is transformed in rich variety in extrauterine life. But it will be *hearing* that gives the newborn its richest experiences.

The mother's voice is now more distinct, though similar enough to what was heard in intrauterine life to give assurance of continuity.

An added and transforming experience is provided by the baby's own voice, which had been muted by the collapsed lungs and the pervasive fluid environment. In seconds all this is changed after birth by the baby's first cry.

Careful studies have shown how essential it is for the baby's well-being and its future mental and emotional life that it be given loving attention immediately onward from the trauma of birth. Four principal experiences give the baby assurance in the exposed conditions of its changed life. First, there is suckling at its mother's breast with all the pleasurable movements and contacts. Second is the mother's voice with all of its charming modulation in "baby talk," the recognized voice from its intrauterine experience. Tests have revealed that a baby recognizes its mother's voice a few days after birth —perhaps even earlier. Doubtless this voice-learning was being accomplished *in utero*. Third, there are all the pleasurable contacts of patting and caresses on the skin, and the movements in response to these. Fourth, there is the visual world, initially centered on the mother's face. Very early the baby recognizes its mother and the facial emotions portrayed in her face. This has been well illustrated in the photographic studies reported by Colwyn Trevarthen.

Let us now look back to consider how it comes about that about the fortieth week of pregnancy birth is induced. It has been natural to assume that such factors as the rapid expansion of the uterus in the last weeks of pregnancy and the nutritional demands of the rapidly growing fetus have initiated the maternal response of endocrine secretions, uterine contractions and eventually abdominal contractions. But much was obscure, and it has remained for Graham Liggins to discover that it is not the mother but the fetus that initiates the birth process to secure its own liberation. At the base of its brain is a large collection of nerve cells, the hypothalamus, that controls the secretion of the hormone called ACTH by the pituitary gland situated just below it. Then begins a complex hormonal series of interactions involving the *prostaglandins,* which pass through the placenta into the maternal circulation. This triggers the maternal processes culminating in birth. As would be expected, if the fetus is anencephalic, lacking a developed forebrain, its birth is indefinitely delayed.

This remarkable discovery is now generally accepted and forms the basis of treatments for disorders of the birth process, for example, delayed births or threatened premature births. Our present point, however, is that the fetus is the initiator. As would be expected, multiple births tend to come on earlier because of the synergism of the summed fetal hormones delivered to the mother.

THE LIFE OF THE BABY

Let us consider first the life of the normal baby. One cannot doubt that it is a consciously perceiving being. It shows a great variety of emotional states: happiness, excitement, fear, anger, frustration, pleasure, pain—all growing in vividness of expression. But on the *continuum* concept, we must recognize that it was conscious long before birth, though limited in its experiences and behavior. Of course we can have no direct awareness of a baby's consciousness, any more than of the consciousness of higher animals, the mammals and birds. But crucial evidence is provided by the recall of our earliest remembered experiences, which have an indelibility because of their severity or their intense emotional associations. One of us can vividly still recall the terrible trauma of being held over the fumes of a gas retort in the Melbourne gas works in order that the sulphur fumes would loosen the flow of the viscid secretions of a near-fatal whooping cough. This happened at just under one year of age. Such remembered episodes of babyhood are certain indications of a continuous consciousness that is largely beyond recall.

Special interest attaches to the prematurely born fetus. With modern therapy, survival and development are possible for a twenty-four-week-old fetus. There are of course disabilities, because a cocoonlike existence is an imperfect substitute for intrauterine security. Its temperature control and its nutritional abilities are both very undeveloped. Yet human beings are extremely adaptable, and we must not be pessimistic about the human life that begins as a prematurely born baby. Every effort must be made to enhance the performance of the life-support equipment for such babies.

One of the most important learning tasks of a baby concerns its recognition of the spatial relations of the visual world. It achieves this initially by the use of its hands. Hand-viewing with hand movements occupies much of its attention in the first weeks of life. So it learns about the spatial relationships of the visually observed hand that it is moving, and then of the relationship of the hand to objects within its reach. At first the movements are clumsy, but by about five months the baby can move its hand effectively to grasp objects. Meanwhile it is learning to crawl so as to explore the contents of the room and to identify visually their explored spatial relationships. In this way each of us has learned to interpret the sensory inputs from the retinal images, which from moment to moment give us the world that we can move in with assurance. In a manner that we do not understand, the baby learns to use its brain in order to bring about the movements that it desires. Throughout life we continue to develop this conscious control of our brains in bringing about voluntary movements (Chapter 11); but it is, in its essentials, an utterly mysterious process.

Long before a baby utters recognizable words it is practicing its vocal organs with the articulation of recognizable *phonemes* that eventually will find expression in the first words: "mama," "papa." Hanus Papousek of Munich has studied baby talk with systematic tape recordings of the stages of its development. It is remarkable that a baby is practicing almost incessantly even when alone. It is learning the complex muscle movements required for making sounds. These movements of larynx, pharynx, tongue, mouth, and respiration are combinations of *motor programs,* to be considered in Chapter 11, that are extremely complex in the production of speech. As described in Chapter 8, the chimpanzee can make a variety of noises but apparently does not have a brain able to learn the motor programs required for speech. In contrast a baby has an inexorable drive to master the making of sounds comparable to those it hears. The deaf baby suffers a great deprivation with no chance to learn these motor programs, and so it falls back on the imperfect but most ingenious sign language for communication. Every effort should be made to provide such children with deaf-aid equipment specially designed to compensate for the hearing loss so that they can learn normal speech instead of sign language.

BABY TO CHILD

We come now to a transcendence in development. After the initial usage of speech to obtain desirables such as food, drink, caressing, movements—the so-called pragmatic speech utterances—the baby-child comes to a different use of speech. It begins to ask questions in the attempt to learn about its outside world and about itself as a participant in that world. This is called *mathetic* speech, and it is peculiarly human (cf. Chapter 8). The baby graduates into childhood as it learns to be a participant in the happenings of the world. Its limited conscious life gives way to the self-conscious life of the human child. It learns, for example, to recognize itself in a mirror at about eighteen months of age.

We can use the term *human being* to cover the whole continuum of human existence from the single-cell zygote through fetal life to the whole of babyhood. With the growing self-consciousness of the child, as indicated by its relationship to other beings like itself—parents, brothers, sisters, friends—it becomes a *human person* with a gradually developing system of values. There is a veritable transcendence from the self-centeredness of the baby to the socially minded child with concepts of rights and duties, now on the threshold of all the rich and wonderful personal relationships that are its birthright. A child has a veritable word hunger as it struggles for self-realization and self-expression. And so we come to Chapter 3, dealing with the human person, and then in Chapter 8, to the theme of human language.

Suggested Readings

ECCLES, J. C. *Facing reality.* Heidelberg: Springer Verlag, 1970, Ch. VI.

ECCLES, J. C. *The human mystery.* Berlin, Heidelberg, New York: Springer Verlag, Chs. IV, V, VII.

GRIFFIN, D. R. *The question of animal awareness.* New York: Rockefeller University Press, 1976.

JERISON, H. J. *Evolution of the brain and intelligence.* New York, London: Academic Press, 1973.

MAYR, E. *Animal species and evolution.* Cambridge, Mass.: Harvard University Press, 1973.

PEACOCKE, A. R. *Science and the Christian experiment.* London: Oxford University Press, 1971.

POPPER, K. R. and ECCLES, J. C. *The self and its brain.* Heidelberg, New York, London: Springer Verlag Internat., 1977, Ch. P1, Dialogues I, II, VIII, X.

STARR, C. (Ed.). *Biology today.* New York: Random House, 1975.

THORPE, W. H. *Animal nature and human nature.* London: Methuen, 1974.

THORPE, W. H. *Purpose in a world of chance: A biologist's view.* Oxford: Oxford University Press, 1978.

VILLEE, C. A. *Biology.* Philadelphia: W. B. Saunders Co., 1972.

WILSON, E. O. *Sociobiology: The new synthesis.* Cambridge, Mass.: The Belknap Press, Harvard University Press, 1975.

3

Self-consciousness and
the Human Person

The Emergence of Self-consciousness

It is proposed to use the term "self-conscious mind" for the highest
mental experiences. It implies knowing that one knows, which is of
course initially a subjective or introspective criterion. However, by
linguistic communication it can be authenticated that other human
beings share in this experience of self-knowing. Dobzhansky expresses well the extraordinary emergence of human self-consciousness—of self-awareness, as he calls it:

> Self-awareness is, then, one of the fundamental, possibly the most fun-
> damental, characteristic of the human species. This characteristic is an
> evolutionary novelty; the biological species from which mankind has
> descended had only rudiments of self-awareness, or perhaps lacked it
> altogether. Self-awareness has, however, brought in its train somber
> companions—fear, anxiety, and death awareness. . . . Man is bur-

dened by death awareness. A being who knows that he will die arose from ancestors who did not know.

This state of ultimate concern devolving from self-awareness can first be identified by the ceremonial burial customs that were inaugurated by Neanderthal man about 80,000 years ago. Karl Popper recognized the unfathomable problem of its origin: "The emergence of all consciousness, capable of self-reflection is indeed one of the greatest of miracles." And Konrad Lorenz refers to "that most mysterious of barriers, utterly impenetrable to the human understanding, that runs through the middle of what is the undeniable oneness of our personality—the barrier that divides our subjective experience from the objective, verifiable physiological events that occur in our body."

The progressive development from the consciousness of the baby to the self-consciousness in the child provides a good model for the emergent evolution of self-consciousness in the hominids. There is even evidence for a primitive knowledge of self with the chimpanzee (but not lower primates) that recognizes itself in a mirror, as shown by the use of the mirror to remove a colored mark on its face. It would seem that, in the evolutionary process, there was some primitive recognition of self long before it became traumatically experienced in death-awareness, which achieved expression in some religious beliefs manifested in the ceremonial burials. Similarly, with the child knowledge of the self usually antedates by years the first experience of death-awareness.

It may be helpful to attempt some diagrammatic representation of the emergence of self-consciousness. In the formal information-flow diagram of brain–mind interaction (Figure 3–1) are three major components of World 2, which is the world of conscious experiences (cf. Figure 3–3). The "outer sense" and "inner sense" compartments are integrated in the central compartment, which may be labeled psyche, self, or soul according to the kind of discourse—psychological, philosophical, or religious. It was conjectured in Chapter 2 that higher animals are conscious, but not self-conscious. Thus the information-flow diagram would be simplified by elimination of the central core as shown in Figure 3–2 with the representation of only the outer sense and inner sense components. The language training of apes has revealed that feelings are dominant in their concentration on the pragmatic use of language for obtaining desirables.* In the

* In Chapter 8, however, we question whether such performances are genuinely linguistic.

evolutionary emergence of self-consciousness David Lack and Konrad Lorenz speak of the unbridgeable gap or gulf between soul and body. Yet we must envisage the creation and development of the central core to give eventually the full emergence of psyche or soul as illustrated in Figure 3–1. It can be conjectured that in the phylogenetic process of hominid evolution were all transitions between the situations illustrated in Figures 3–2 and 3–1, just as occurs ontogenetically from human baby to human child to human adult; yet it remains a miracle.

The Human Person

Each of us continually has the experience of being a person with a self-consciousness not just conscious, but knowing that we know. In

FIGURE 3–1.   Information Flow Diagram for Brain–Mind Interaction in Human Brain. The three components of World 2—outer sense, inner sense, and the psyche, self, or soul—are diagrammed, with their communications shown by arrows. Also shown are the lines of communication across the interface between World 1 and World 2, that is, from the liaison brain to and from these World 2 components. The liaison brain has the columnar arrangement indicated by the vertical broken lines. It must be imagined that the area of the liaison brain is enormous, with open or active modules numbering over a million, not just the two score here depicted.

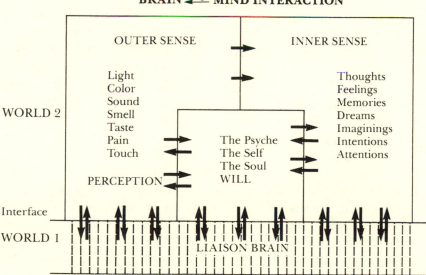

BRAIN ⇌ MIND INTERACTION

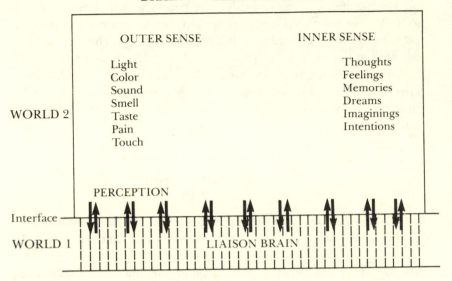

FIGURE 3-2. Information Flow Diagram for Brain–Mind Interaction for a Mammalian Brain. The two components of World 2, outer sense and inner sense, are diagrammed, with communications shown by arrows to the liaison brain in World 1. It will be noticed that mammals are given a World 2, corresponding to their consciousness, and that this World 2 has the same general features in outer sense and inner sense as with the human World 2 in Figure 3–1, but there is a complete absence of the central category of psyche, self, or soul.

defining "person" I shall quote two admirable statements by Immanuel Kant: "A person is a subject who is responsible for his actions" and "A person is something that is conscious at different times of the numerical identity of its self." These statements are minimal and basic, and they should be enormously expanded. For example Popper and Eccles have recently published a six-hundred-page book on *The Self and its Brain*. On page 144 Popper refers to "that greatest of miracles: the human consciousness of self."

We are not able to go much farther than Kant in defining the relations of the person to its brain. We are apt to regard the person as identical with the ensemble of face, body, limbs, and the rest that constitute each of us. It is easy to show that this is a mistake. Amputation of limbs or loss of eyes, for example, though crippling, leaves the human person with its essential identity. This is also the case with the removal of internal organs. Many can be excised in whole or in part. The human person survives unchanged after kidney transplants or even heart transplants. You may ask what happens with brain transplants. Mercifully this is not feasible surgically, but even now it would be possible successfully to accomplish a head transplant. Who can doubt that the person "owning" the transplanted head would now "own" the acquired body, and not vice versa! We can hope that with human persons this will remain a Gedanken experiment, but it has already been successfully done in mammals. We can recognize that all structures of the head extraneous to the brain are not involved in this transplanted ownership. For example eyes, nose, jaws, scalp, and so forth are no more concerned than are other parts of the body. So we can conclude that it is the brain and the brain alone that provides the material basis of our personhood.

But when we come to consider the brain as the seat of the conscious personhood, we can also recognize that large parts of the brain are not essential. For example removal of the cerebellum gravely incapacitates movement, but the person is not otherwise affected. It is quite different with the main part of the brain, the cerebral hemispheres. They are intimately related to the consciousness of the person, but not equally. In 95 percent of persons there is dominance of the left hemisphere, which is the "speaking hemisphere." Except in infants its removal results in a most severe destruction of the human person, but not annihilation. On the other hand removal of the minor hemisphere (usually the right) is attended with loss of movement on the left side (hemiplegia) and blindness on the left side (hemianopia), but the person is otherwise not gravely disturbed. Damage to other parts of the brain can also greatly disturb the human personhood, possibly by the removal of the neural inputs that normally generate the necessary background activity of the cerebral hemispheres. The most tragic example is vigil coma in which enduring deep unconsciousness is caused by damage to the midbrain.

The Human Person and World 3

The three-world philosophy of Popper forms the basis of our further exploration of the way in which a human baby becomes a human person. As shown in Figure 3–3, all the material world including even human brains is in the matter–energy World 1. World 2 is the world of all conscious experiences (cf. Figure 3–1). By contrast, World 3 is the world of knowledge in the objective sense, and as such has an extremely wide range of contents. Figure 3–3 offers an abbreviated list.

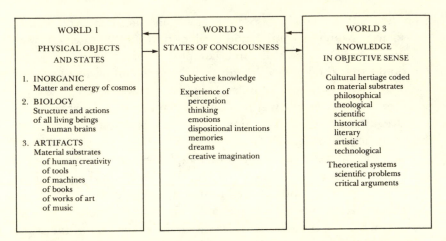

WORLD 1	WORLD 2	WORLD 3
PHYSICAL OBJECTS AND STATES	STATES OF CONSCIOUSNESS	KNOWLEDGE IN OBJECTIVE SENSE
1. INORGANIC Matter and energy of cosmos 2. BIOLOGY Structure and actions of all living beings - human brains 3. ARTIFACTS Material substrates of human creativity of tools of machines of books of works of art of music	Subjective knowledge Experience of perception thinking emotions dispositional intentions memories dreams creative imagination	Cultural hertiage coded on material substrates philosophical theological scientific historical literary artistic technological Theoretical systems scientific problems critical arguments

FIGURE 3–3. Tabular Representation of the Contents of the Three Worlds in Accordance with the Philosophy of Karl Popper. These three worlds are nonoverlapping but are intimately related, as indicated by the large open arrows at the top. They contain everything in existence and in experience. World 1 is material, Worlds 2 and 3 are immaterial.

For example World 3 comprises the expressions of scientific, literary, and artistic ideas that have been preserved in codified form in libraries, in museums, and in all records of human culture. In their material composition of paper and ink, books are in World 1, but the knowledge encoded in the print is in World 3, and similarly for pictures, sculptures, and all other artifacts such as musical scores. Most important components of World 3 are languages for communicating thoughts (cf. Chapter 8) and a system of values for regulating conduct (Chapters 5 and 6) and also arguments generated by discussion of these problems. In summary it can be stated that World 3 comprises the records of the intellectual efforts of all mankind through all ages up to the present—what we may call the cultural heritage.

At birth the human baby has a human brain, but its World 2 experiences are quite rudimentary, and World 3 is unknown to it. It, and even a human embryo, must be regarded as human beings, but not as human persons.* The emergence and development of self-consciousness (World 2) by continued interaction with World 3, the world of culture, is an utterly mysterious process. It can be likened to a double structure (Figure 3–4) that ascends and grows by effective

* A being must be regarded as a *human* being when its genetic constitution (genotype) is formed from the gene pool of *Homo sapiens*. A human being graduates to be a *person* on less specific and more arguable grounds, e.g. when it displays certain social, moral, and intellectual attributes, or that of self-conscious reflection.

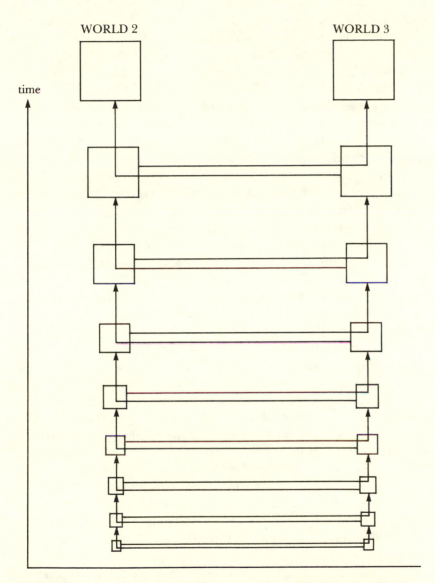

FIGURE 3-4.   Diagrammatic Representation of the Postulated Inter-relationships in the Developments of Self-consciousness (World 2) and of Culture (World 3) of a Person in Time. Development is shown by the arrows; full description in text. We may call it the ladder of personhood that we can climb up throughout life.

cross-linkage. The vertical arrow shows the passage of time from the earliest experiences of the child up to full human development. From each World 2 position an arrow leads through to World 3 at that level up to a higher, larger level, which illustrates symbolically a growth in the culture of that individual. Reciprocally the World 3 resources of the self act back to give a higher, expanded level of consciousness of that self (World 2). Figure 3–4 can be regarded symbolically as the ladder of personhood. And so each of us has developed progressively in self-creation, and this can go on throughout our whole lifetime. The more the World 3 resources of the human person, the more does it gain in the self-consciousness of World 2 by reciprocal enrichment. What we are is dependent on the World 3 that we have been immersed in and how effectively we have utilized our opportunities to make the most of our brain potentialities.

A recent tragic case is illustrative of Figure 3–4. A child, Genie, was deprived of all World 3 influences by her psychotic father. She was penned in isolation in a small room of his house in Los Angeles, never spoken to, and minimally serviced from the age of twenty months up to thirteen years, eight months. On release from this terrible deprivation she was of course a human being, but not a human person. She was at the bottom rung of the ladder in Figure 3–4. Since then, with dedicated help by Dr. Susan Curtiss, she has been slowly climbing up that ladder of personhood for the last ten years. The linguistic deprivation seriously damaged her left hemisphere, but the right hemisphere stands in for a much-depleted language performance. Yet, despite this terribly delayed immersion in World 3, Genie has become a human person with self-consciousness, emotions, and excellent performances in manual dexterity and in visual recognition. We can recognize the necessity of World 3 for the development of the human person. As illustrated in Figure 6–1, the brain is built by genetic instructions (that is, Nature), but development of human personhood is dependent on World 3 environment (that is, Nurture). With Genie there was a gap of thirteen years between Nature and Nurture.

It may seem that a complete explanation of the development of the human person can be given in terms of the human brain. It is built anatomically by genetic instructions (Chapter 2) and subsequently developed functionally by learning from the environmental influences (Chapter 9). A purely materialist explanation would seem to suffice with the conscious experiences as derivative from brain functioning. However, it is a mistake to think that the brain does everything and that our conscious experiences are simply a reflection of brain activities, which is a common philosophical view. If that were so, our conscious selves would be no more than passive spectators of the performances carried out by the neuronal mechanisms of the brain. Our beliefs that we can really make decisions and that we have some control over our actions (Chapters 5 and 11) would be nothing but illusions. There are, of course, all sorts of subtle cover-ups by philosophers from such a stark exposition, but they do not face up to the issue. In fact all people, even materialist philosophers, behave as if they had at least some responsibility for their own actions. It seems that their philosophy is for "the other people, not for themselves," as Schopenhauer wittily stated.

These considerations lead me to the alternative hypothesis of dualist-interactionism (cf. Figure 3–1), which has been expanded at length in *The Self and its Brain*. It is really the commonsense view, namely, that we are a combination of two things or entities: our brains on the one hand; and our conscious selves on the other. The self is central to the totality of our conscious experiences as persons through our whole waking life. We link it in memory from our earliest conscious experiences. The self has a subconscious existence during sleep, except for dreams, and on waking the conscious self is resumed and linked with the past by the continuity of memory. But for memory we as experiencing persons would not exist, as will be made apparent in Chapter 9. We have the extraordinary problem that was first recognized by Descartes: How can the conscious mind and the brain interact?

Hypotheses Relating to the Brain–Mind Problem

Chapter 4 is reserved for an accessible but not exhausted treatment of the philosophical literature on the "brain-mind" or "mind-body" problem. A thorough treatment has been provided in a masterful manner by Popper in the recent book *The Self and its Brain*. He has critically surveyed the historical development of the problem from the earliest records of Greek thought. We can begin by a simple illustration (Figure 3–5) of the principal varieties of these complex and subtle philosophies, concentrating specifically on the formulations that relate to the brain rather than the body, because clinical neurology

DIAGRAMMATIC REPRESENTATION OF BRAIN–MIND THEORIES

World 1 = All of material or physical world including brains
World 2 = All subjective or mental experiences
World 1_P is all the material world that is without mental states
World 1_M is that minute fraction of the material world with associated
        mental states

Radical Materialism:	World 1 = World 1_P; World 1_M = 0; World 2 = 0.
Panpsychism:	All is World 1–2, World 1 or 2 does not exist alone.
Epiphenomenalism:	World 1 = World 1_P + World 1_M
	World $1_M \rightarrow$ World 2
Identity Theory:	World 1 = World 1_P + World 1_M
	World 1_M = World 2 (the identity)
Dualist-Interactionism:	World 1 = World 1_P + World 1_M
	World $1_M \rightleftharpoons$ World 2; this interaction occurs in the liaison brain, LB = World 1_M
	Thus World 1 = World 1_P + World 1_{LB}, and World $1_{LB} \rightleftharpoons$ World 2

FIGURE 3-5. Diagrammatic Representation of Brain-Mind Theories. Diagram incorporates the World 1 and World 2 of Figure 3-3. The essential features of the materialist theories of the mind are summarized for panpsychism, epiphenomenalism, and the identity theory. This last theory has a variety of names according to the whims of the creators of the minor varieties of what are essentially parallelist theories. The subdivision of World 1 into World 1_P and World 1_M helps in clarification of their specific features. World 1_M is assumed to be restricted to special states of the brain in epiphenomenalism, the identity theory, and dualist-interactionism. The essential and unique feature of dualist-interactionism is shown by the reciprocal arrows between World 1_M and World 2 in the second line.

and the neurosciences make it abundantly clear that the mind has no direct access to the body. All interactions with the body are mediated by the brain, and furthermore only by the higher levels of cerebral activity.

     The theories of the brain–mind relationship that are today held by most philosophers and neuroscientists are purely materialistic in the sense that the brain is given complete mastery! The existence of mind or consciousness is not denied except by radical materialists (cf. Figure 3–5), but it is relegated to the passive role of mental experiences accompanying some types of brain action, as in epiphenomenalism and in psychoneural identity (cf. Figure 3–5), but with absolutely no *effective* action on the brain. The complex neural mechanism of the brain functions in its determined materialistic fashion regardless of any consciousness that may accompany it. The "commonsense" experiences that we can control our actions to some extent (cf.Chapter 11) or that indicate we can express our thoughts in language (Chapter 8) are alleged to be illusory. An *effective causality* is denied to the self-conscious mind *per se* despite all the protests of the materialists to the contrary!

In contrast to these materialist or parallelist theories are the *dualist-interaction* theories (Figure 3–5). The essential feature of these theories is that mind and brain are independent entities, the brain being in World 1 and the mind in World 2, and that they somehow interact, as illustrated by the arrows in Figure 3–1. Thus there is a frontier, as diagrammed in Figure 3–1, and across this frontier there is interaction in both directions, which can be conceived as a flow of information, not of energy. Thus we have the extraordinary doctrine that the world of matter–energy (World 1) is not completely sealed, which is a fundamental tenet of physics, but that there are small "apertures" in what is otherwise the completely closed World 1. On the contrary, the closedness of World 1 has been safeguarded with great ingenuity in all materialist theories of the mind. We shall later argue that this is not their strength but instead their fatal weakness.

Neuroscientists find the identity theory in one or another of its many guises attractive because it gives the future to them. It is admitted that our present understanding of the brain is quite inadequate to provide more than a crude explanation of how the brain delivers all the richness and wonderful variety of perceptual experiences, or how the mental events or thoughts can have the immense range and fruitfulness that our imaginative insights achieve in their action on the world. However, all this is taken care of by the theory that has been named *promissory materialism* by Popper. This theory derives from the great successes of the neurosciences, which undoubtedly are disclosing more and more of what is happening in the brain, in perception, in memory, in the control of movement, and in states of consciousness and unconsciousness (Chapters 9 and 11). The aim of these research programs is to give a more and more complete and coherent account of the manner in which the total performance and experience of an animal and of a human being are explicable by the action of the neural mechanisms of the brain. According to the promissory materialist this scientific advance will progressively restrict the phenomena that appear to require mental terms for their explanation so that in the fullness of time everything will be describable in the materialist terms of the neurosciences. The victory of materialism over mentalism will be complete.

As Popper states:

> The victory is to come about as follows. With the progress of brain
> research, the language of the physiologists is likely to penetrate more
> and more into ordinary language and to change our picture of the
> universe, including that of common sense. So we shall be talking less
> and less about experiences, perceptions, thoughts, beliefs, purposes
> and aims; and more and more about brain processes, about disposi-
> tions to behave, and about overt behavior. In this way mentalist
> language will go out of fashion and be used only in historical reports, or
> metaphorically, or ironically. When this stage has been reached, men-
> talism will be stone-dead, and the problem of mind in relation to the
> body will have solved itself. In support of promissory materialism it is
> pointed out that this is exactly what has happened in the case of the
> problem of witches and their relation to the devil. If at all, we now
> speak of witches either to characterize an archaic superstition, or we
> speak ironically or metaphorically. The same will happen with mind
> language, we are promised: perhaps not so *very* soon—perhaps not
> even during the life span of the present generation—but soon enough.

We regard promissory materialism as a superstition without a
rational foundation. The more we discover about the brain, the more
clearly do we distinguish between the brain events and the mental
phenomena, and the more wonderful do both the brain events and
the mental phenomena become. Promissory materialism is simply a
religious belief held by dogmatic materialists such as Mario Bunge,
who often confuse their religion with their science. It has all the
features of a messianic prophecy—the promise of a future freed of all
problems, a kind of Nirvana for our unfortunate successors, as is
ironically described by Gunter Stent in his book *The Coming of the
Golden Age*. In contrast the true scientific attitude as described by Popper is that scientific problems are unending in providing challenges to
attain an ever wider and deeper understanding of nature and of
ourselves.

Critical Evaluation of
Brain-Mind Hypotheses

A great point is made by all varieties of materialists that their brain-
mind theories (Figure 3-5) are in accord with natural law as it now
stands. However, this claim is invalidated by two most weighty considerations.

First, nowhere in the laws of physics or in the laws of the derivative sciences, chemistry and biology, is there any reference to consciousness or mind. Regardless of the complexity of electrical, chemical, or biological machinery, there is no statement in the "natural laws" that there is an emergence of this strange nonmaterial entity, consciousness or mind (cf. Chapter 2). This is not to affirm that consciousness does not emerge in the evolutionary process, but merely to state that its emergence is not reconcilable with the natural laws as at present understood. For example such laws do not allow any statement that consciousness emerges at a specified level of complexity of systems, which is gratuitously assumed by all materialists except radical materialists and panpsychists. The panpsychist belief that some primordial consciousness attaches to all matter, presumably even to atoms and subatomic particles, finds no support whatsoever in physics. One can also recall the poignant questions by computer lovers: At what stage of complexity and performance can we agree to endow them with consciousness? Mercifully this emotionally charged question need not be answered. You can do what you like to computers without qualms of being cruel!

Second, all materialist theories of the mind are in conflict with biological evolution. Since they all (panpsychists, epiphenomenalists, and identity theorists) assert the causal ineffectiveness of consciousness *per se* (Figure 3-5), they fail completely to account for the evolutionary expansion of consciousness, which is an undeniable fact. There is first its emergence and then its progressive development with the growing complexity of the brain. Evolutionary theory holds that only those structures and processes that significantly aid in survival are developed in natural selection. If consciousness is causally impotent, its development cannot be accounted for by evolutionary theory. According to biological evolution, mental states and consciousness could have evolved and developed *only if they were causally effective* in bringing about changes in neural happenings in the brain with the consequent changes in behavior. That can occur only if the neural machinery of the brain is open to influences from the mental events of the world of conscious experiences, which is the basic postulate of dualist–interactionist theory.

Finally, the most telling criticism of all materialist theories of the mind is against its key postulate that the happenings in the neural machinery of the brain provide *a necessary and sufficient explanation of the totality both of the performance and of the conscious experience of a human being.* For example the willing of a voluntary movement (Chapter 11) is regarded as being *completely determined* by events in the neural machinery of the brain, as also are all other cognitive experiences. But as Popper states in his Compton Lecture:

> According to determinism, any such theory such as say determinism is held because of a certain physical structure of the holder—perhaps of his brain. Accordingly, we are deceiving ourselves and are physically so determined as to deceive ourselves whenever we believe that there are such things as *arguments or reasons* which make us accept determinism. Purely physical conditions, including our physical environment make us say or accept whatever we say or accept.

This is an effective *reductio ad absurdum*. This stricture applies to all of the materialist theories. So perforce we turn to dualist–interactionist explanations of the brain–mind problem, despite the extraordinary requirement that there be effective communication in both directions across the frontier shown in Figure 3–1.

Necessarily the dualist–interactionist theory is in conflict with present natural laws and so is in the same "unlawful" position as the materialist theories of the mind. The differences are that this conflict has always been admitted and that the neural machinery of the brain is assumed to operate in strict accordance to natural laws except for its openness to World 2 influences.

Moreover, as Popper stated, the interaction across the frontier in Figure 3–1 need not be in conflict with the first law of thermodynamics. The flow of information into the modules could be effected by a balanced increase and decrease of energy at different but adjacent micro-sites, so that there is no net energy change in the brain. The first law at this level may be valid only statistically.

The Human Brain

It is useful to think of the brain as an instrument, our computer, which has been a lifelong servant and companion. It provides us, as programmers, with the lines of communication from and to the material world (World 1) which comprises both our bodies and the external world. It does this by receiving information through the immense sensory system of millions of nerve fibers that fire impulses into the brain, where it is processed into the coded patterns of information that we read out from moment to moment in deriving all our experiences—our percepts, thoughts, ideas, memories. But we as experiencing persons do not slavishly accept all that is provided for us by our computer, the neuronal structures of our sensory system and of our brain. We select from all that is given according to interest and attention, and we modify the actions of the neuronal structures of our computer, for example to initiate some willed movement or in order to recall a memory or to concentrate our attention.

How then can we develop ideas with respect to the mode of operation of the brain? How can it provide the immense range of coded information that can be selected from by the mind in its activity of reading our conscious experiences? It is now possible to give much more informative answers because of very recent work on the essential mode of operation of the neocortex. By the use of radiotracer techniques it has been shown that the great brain mantle, the neocortex, is built up of units or modules. This modular organization has provided most valuable simplification of the enterprise of trying to understand how this tremendously complex structure works. The potential performance of a network of ten thousand million individual nerve cells is beyond all comprehension. The arrangement in modules of about four thousand nerve cells each reduces the number of functional units of the neocortex to between 2 and 3 million.

It can be asked, however, whether 2 to 3 million modules of the neocortex are adequate to generate the spatiotemporal patterns that encode the total cognitive performance of the human brain—all the sensing, all memories, all linguistic expression, all creativities, all aesthetic experiences—for our whole lifetime. The only answer I can give is to refer to the immense potentialities of the eighty-eight keys of a piano. Think of the creative performances of the great piano composers, Beethoven and Chopin for example. They could use only four parameters in their creation of piano music with the eighty-eight keys, each of which has an invariant pitch and tonal quality. And a comparable four parameters are used in creating the spatiotemporal patterns of activity in the 2 to 3 million modules of the human cerebral cortex.

I think it will be recognized that the enormous generation of musical patterns using the eighty-eight keys of a piano points to a virtually infinite capacity of the 2 to 3 million modules to generate unique spatiotemporal patterns. Moreover it must be realized that these patterns giving the conscious experiences are dependent on the same four parameters as for the piano keys. We can imagine that the intensities of activation are signaled symbolically by the momentary lighting up of modules. So, if we could see the surface of our neocortex, it would present illuminated patterns of 50 cm by 50 cm in area composed at any moment of modules 0.3 mm across that have all ranges of "openness" from dark to dim to lighter to brilliant. And this pattern would be changing in a scintillating manner from moment to moment, giving a sparkling spatiotemporal pattern of the millions of modules that would appear exactly as on a TV screen. This symbolism gives some idea of the immense task confronting the mind in generating conscious experiences. The dark or dim modules would be neglected. Moreover it is an important feature of the hypothesis of mind–brain interaction that neither the mind nor the brain is passive in the transaction. There must be an active interchange of information across the frontier (Figure 3–1) between the material brain—the liaison brain—and the nonmaterial mind. The mind is not in the matter-energy world, so there can be no energy exchange in the transaction, merely a flow of information. Yet the mind must be able to change the pattern of energy operations in the modules of the brain, else it would be forever impotent.

It is difficult to understand how the self-conscious mind can relate to such an enormous complexity of spatiotemporal modular patterns. This difficulty is mitigated by three considerations. First, we must realize that our self-conscious mind has been learning to accomplish such tasks from our babyhood onward, a process that is colloquially called "learning to use one's brain." Second, by the process of attention the self-conscious mind selects from the total ensemble of modular patterns those features that are in accord with its present interests. Third, the self-conscious mind is engaged in extracting "meaning" from all that it reads out. This is well illustrated by the many ambiguous figures, for example a drawing that can be seen either as a staircase or an overhanging cornice. The switch from one interpretation to the other is instantaneous and holistic. There is never any transitional phase in the reading out by the mind of the modular pattern in the brain.

A key component of the hypothesis of brain–mind interaction is that the unity of conscious experience is provided by the self-conscious mind and not by the neuronal mechanism of the neocortex. Hitherto it has been impossible to develop any theory of brain function that would explain how the immense diversity of brain events comes to be synthesized so that there is a unity of conscious experience. The brain events remain disparate, being essentially the individual actions of countless modules.

The Unity of the Self

It is a universal human experience that subjectively there is a mental unity recognized as a continuity from one's earliest memories. It is the basis of the concept of the self. Experimental investigations on the unity of the self have been discussed in the book *The Human Psyche* (Eccles, 1980).

As Robinson has shown elsewhere,* there are insuperable objections to equating the self with memory or the continuity of memories. A total amnesic may not know *who* he is (or anything about his previous life) but he surely knows *that* he is and, therefore, that he is in possession of selfhood. It is, moreover, not the fact that a person recalls having done something that establishes that he, in fact, did it, for memories can be defective and even illusory. Thus the self is certainly not identical with memory. It becomes necessary, then, to make distinctions among three different concepts: *self, self-identity,* and *personal identity.* The self and its unity arise from the irreducible awareness of being. One is aware *that* he is and knows directly that all his experiences, memories, thoughts, and desires inhere in this very self. *Self-identity,* however, refers to the knowledge one has of *who* he is and arises chiefly from memory. Thus, a given (amnesic) self can be lacking in self-identity. *Personal identity,* on the other hand, refers to the knowledge others have of who a given person is. We may say, for example, that a total stranger has no personal identity (as far as we know) although he may well have self-identity. The totally amnesic person who is also a total stranger thus lacks both personal identity and self-identity but possesses selfhood nonetheless. Accordingly, such striking conditions as those popularized in *The Three Faces of Eve* pertain not to the existence of three *selves* in one person but to three distinct *self-identities* possessed by one otherwise unique and irreducible *self.*

By far the most important experimental evidence relating to the unity of consciousness comes from the study by Roger Sperry and his associates on commissurotomized patients. In the operation for the relief of intractable epilepsy there was a section of the corpus callosum, the great tract of nerve fibers, about 200 million, that links the two cerebral hemispheres. With the most sophisticated investigations, allowing up to two hours of continual testing, it became clear

---

* Daniel N. Robinson, "Cerebral Plurality and the Unity of Self," *American Psychologist,* August 1982.

that the right hemisphere, the so-called minor hemisphere, was cor-
related with conscious responses at a level superior to those exhibited
by any nonhuman primates. The patient's consciousness was indubitable. The perplexing question is whether the right hemisphere
mediates self-consciousness, meaning that it permits the knowledge
of selfhood. In the most searching investigations of Sperry and
associates there was testing of the ability of the patient to identify photographs projected to the right hemisphere alone. A considerable ability was displayed, but it was handicapped by the lack of
verbal expression.

The tests for the existence of self-consciousness were at a
relatively simple pictorial and emotional level. We can doubt if the
right hemisphere with associated consciousness has a full self-
conscious existence. For example, do planning and worrying about
the future take place there? Are there decisions and judgments based
on some value system? These are essential qualifications for personhood as ordinarily understood and for the existence of a psyche or
soul. It can be concluded that a limited self-consciousness is
associated with the right hemisphere, but the person remains apparently unscathed by the commissurotomy with mental unity intact
in its now exclusive left hemisphere association. After commissurotomy the right hemisphere appears to mediate a self-
awareness resembling that of a very young child. The information
flow diagram for the right hemisphere would resemble Figure 3–2,
except that there would be a small central core at a primitive level of
self or ego, but with no representation of soul or psyche or personhood. It is generally agreed that the human person is not split by
the commissurotomy but remains in liaison with the left (speaking)
hemisphere.

The Uniqueness of Each Self

It is not in doubt that each human person recognizes its own uniqueness, and this is accepted as the basis of social life and of law.
When we inquire into the grounds for this belief, modern neuros-
cience eliminates an explanation in terms of the body. There remain
two possible alternatives, the brain and the psyche. Materialists must
subscribe to the former, but dualist–interactionists have to regard the
self of World 2 (cf. Figure 3–1) as the entity with the experienced uniqueness. It is important to disclaim a solipsistic solution of the uni-

queness of the self. Our direct experiences are of course subjective, being derived entirely from our brain and self. The existence of other selves is established by intersubjective communication.

If one's experienced uniqueness is attributed to the uniqueness of our brain, built by the unique genetic instructions provided by one's genome, one is confronted by the infinitely improbable genetic lottery (even $10^{10,000}$ against) from which one's genome was derived,* as has been argued by Jennings, by Eccles, and by Thorpe. There is further the impossibility of accounting for the experienced uniqueness of each identical twin despite the identical genome. A frequent and superficially plausible answer to this enigma is the assertion that the determining factor is the uniqueness of the accumulated experiences of a self throughout its lifetime. It is readily agreed that our behavior and memories, and in fact the whole content of our inner conscious life, are dependent on the accummulated experiences of our lives, but no matter how extreme the change at some particular decision point produced by the exigencies of circumstances, one would still be the same self able to trace back one's continuity in memory to the earliest remembrances at the age of one year or so, the same self in a quite other guise. There could be no elimination of a self and creation of a new self!

Since materialist solutions fail to account for our experienced uniqueness, we are constrained to attribute the uniqueness of the psyche or soul to a supernatural spiritual creation. To give the explanation in theological terms: Each soul is a Divine creation, which is "attached" to the growing fetus at some time between conception and birth. It is the certainty of the inner core of unique individuality that necessitates the "Divine creation." We submit that no other explanation is tenable; neither the genetic uniqueness with its fantastically impossible lottery nor the environmental differentiations, which do not *determine* one's uniqueness but merely modify it.

* This probability argument has been criticized by Willem Kuijk in *An Outline of a Complementarial Philosophy of Science with Special Reference to Mathematics,* forthcoming. His argument is simply that *after* a particular event the chance of its occurrence is 100 percent, and this holds true for one's own unique existence despite the odds that could be calculated, $10^{10,000}$ against, before that existence was realized. We reply that this refutation is inapplicable. We are not arguing about "myself" as *observed objectively* with "my body" and its behavior including verbal utterances as witnessed by an observer. We are in a completely different logical world when it is *self-experienced uniqueness* that is at issue, as can be gathered from the arguments presented in *The Human Psyche* on pages 237 to 241. This uniqueness is not objectively recognized by an observer. On the contrary, the argument is for the existence of myself known only to myself. One can image the extreme improbability of one's existence if it was dependent on the genetic code. *Before* it came to pass it would be $10^{10,000}$ against.

An appealing analogy is to regard the body and brain as a superb computer built by genetic coding that has been created by the wonderful process of biological evolution. On the analogy, the soul or psyche is the programmer of the computer. Each of us as a programmer is born with our computer in its initial embryonic state. We develop it throughout life, as is indicated in Figure 3-4. It is our lifelong intimate companion in all transactions. It receives from and gives to the world, which includes other selves. The great mysteries are in our creation as programmers or experiencing selves and in our association throughout life, each person with its own computer, as is diagrammed in Figure 3-1 across the frontier between World 2 and World 1.

Yet even in saying this perhaps we give too much away to the biological or scientific perspective and say too little of the striking dilemmas and confusions that stalk even the most modest of materialistic accounts. Let us next examine versions of these accounts as they seek to reduce both mind and self to the more ordinary (material) contents of the physical world.

Suggested Readings

BELOFF, J. *The existence of mind.* London: MacGibbon & Kee, 1962.

BLAKEMORE C. *Mechanics of the mind.* Cambridge, London: Cambridge University Press, 1977.

ECCLES, J. C. *Facing reality.* Heidelberg: Springer Verlag, 1970, Chs. 4,5,6,10.

ECCLES, J. C. *The human mystery.* Heidelberg: Springer Verlag, 1979, Chs. 6,7,8,10.

ECCLES, J. C. *The human psyche.* Berlin, Heidelberg, New York: Springer Internat., 1980, Chs. 1,2,3,4,7.

GRANIT, R. *The purposive brain.* Cambridge, Mass.: MIT Press, 1977.

LORENZ, K. *Behind the mirror.* London: Methuen & Co., 1977.

PEACOCKE, A. R. *Science and the Christian experiment.* London: Oxford University Press, 1971.

PENFIELD, W. *The mystery of the mind.* Princeton, N.J.: Princeton University Press, 1975.

POPPER, K. R., and ECCLES, J. C. *The self and its brain.* Berlin, Heidelberg, New York: Springer Internat., 1977, Chs.P2,P3,P4,P5,E2, E5, E7, Dialogues II, IV, V, VI, VIII.

ROBINSON, D. Cerebral plurality and the unity of self. *American Psychologist,* August 1982, *37,* 904–910.

SPERRY, R. *Science and moral priority.* New York: Columbia University Press, 1983.

THORPE, W. H. *Animal nature and human nature.* London: Methuen & Co., 1974.

4

Materialism and the Liar's Paradox

In the well-known "liar's paradox" we are confronted by a person who claims, "I *never* tell the truth." We may choose to treat this claim as if it, too, is a lie, but this then requires us to accept the claimant's other utterances as truthful. Or, accepting that indeed he *never* tells the truth, we must take his admission as contradictory, for at least in the admission we have one instance of truth-telling.

Something similarly paradoxical occurs when a person claims to be no more than a special kind of purely material organization, a kind of machine, which, though complex, it totally governed and explained by the laws of the physical sciences. If we ask him if in fact he *believes* he is a machine and *expects* us to take his word for it, his reply will establish that he has beliefs and expectations. Related questions will no doubt establish further that he has hopes, convictions, consciousness, feelings, needs, theories, and all the other states or conditions ordinarily reserved either to living things or to human beings alone. As with the liar's paradox, it is not entirely clear how we are to understand a fellow being who claims to be a robot, which, after all, is what the radical psychological materialist finally is claiming. A robot is a device constructed to mimic the actions of those we have taken to be persons. The robot's behavior is entirely explicable in the language of physical science, at least in principle. To account for its actions we need not speak of consciousness, intentions, free will, belief, sentiments, and the like. We could construct such a device so that its cheeks would redden when it erred (suggesting "embarrassment") and its face became expressionless in the presence of the unexpected (suggesting "doubt" and "deliberation"). Presumably, we could even program the robot to announce that it possessed a *soul* and to describe it as an immaterial *essence* responsible for all the robot's rational powers and of such a nature as to survive the destruction of the robot's material parts.

It should be quite obvious that anything we might point to as a sign of the uniqueness of human life can be recast in the radical materialist's idiom. To the extent that consciousness is identical to the *report* of consciousness, any robot reporting to be conscious would qualify. And the same would be true of feelings, convictions, and the balance of our psychological attributes. The advocate of materialism, when challenged by the extraordinary achievements of the human race, can always defend his thesis by declaring that, although no current machine can accomplish such feats, there is no reason *in principle* why future machines will not.

It is important to recognize that theories of this kind are not scientific but metaphysical. They can be weighed only according to logic and syntax, not against the standards of scientific testing and measurement. Our protagonist could make precisely the same claims about trees, carpets, hamsters, or paperweights. How, after all, could one *prove* that a paperweight lacks consciousness and feeling? And might not trees express poetic genius if only they had mouths and vocal cords? As long as we refuse to admit into the debate the forever *private* awareness each person has of himself, his thoughts and feelings, his judgments and rationality, and as long as we insist on public and purely behavioral signs of these, radical materialism can remain in the debate. It will always defend itself against hard cases by relying on certain anatomical nuances (human beings have hands and hamsters don't) or on the argument of "complexity" (hamsters are different from persons because they are materially simpler in their organization).

Although philosophical *pragmatism* suffers any number of liabilities, it offers at least one helpful hint as we set about to weigh a thesis such as this. One of pragmatism's chief tenets, often referred to as the "pragmatic theory of truth," is that every metaphysical claim must submit to this question: How would the actual facts, states, and conditions of the real world, including our relationship to these facts, states, and conditions, be affected were a particular metaphysical thesis to be true? When we submit the claims of radical materialism to this test, the outcome is surprising: *Nothing changes!* If we accept all of our psychological attributes as being no more than the product of utterly material processes, the attributes remain precisely what they have always been. Our lives are still marked by thoughts, feelings. hopes, confusions, moral dilemmas, aesthetic experiences, and episodes of dark doubt and deep faith. That somehow "in principle" it might be possible to manufacture devices possessing the same attributes is really quite beside the point. All this would do is increase the number of "beings" whose natures we cannot explain. Since we do not know *how* consciousness arises in human beings, the creation of a device that *claims* to be conscious would only add to our ignorance by extending it into the realm of conscious machines.

From a pragmatic perspective we see that radical materialism can be accepted or rejected without consequence. To tell a man grieving over the loss of a loved one that it is possible to make a robot capable of the same grief is to engage in babble, no less rude for being babble. To explain to a jurist that his anguished analysis of the law, his relentless search for *justice* in a given cause, must be understood as the "processing functions" of his nervous system cannot possibly affect either the issue or his jural reasoning.

There may be some who think that the thesis is consequential because, if true, it obliges us to be far more modest about the sorts of beings we are, far more "realistic," far less "judgmental." But what could it possibly mean to say that a group of robots is now under an *obligation* to be modest, realistic, and forgiving? One does not *appeal* to a robot, one merely rewires or reprograms it. On the materialist's thesis, the rewiring and new programming can be accomplished only by other machines (since we're all machines), but this can only take place after some of the machines have discovered that they (we) are all machines after all. We might ask, however, how it was that machines ever thought they were otherwise. To answer that that's how they were programmed is scarcely informative. There must have been an initial programmer (a Prime Mover?), aware of the distinction between machines and human beings, who decided that it would be better for us to believe (!) we are not machines. However, it could not actually be "better" for us so to believe since, as we have shown, it really makes no difference. The facts of human life remain unaltered as we move from one metaphysical thesis to the next. Indeed, even the *religious* dimensions of human life are untouched as long as the facts of our lives remain unaltered. This can be shown—in an appropriately "mechanical" way—through an abridged but suggestive line of argument:

1. I *believe* some of my actions are freely taken.
2. Some credibly free actions affect others in important ways.
3. Such actions are judged by me to be *morally* weighted.
4. There is an ultimate judgment to be made of my worth according to those actions I took to be "free" and morally weighty.
5. Any being—including a manufactured one—for which 1 through 4 are possible falls within the boundaries of faith and salvation.

Note then that radical materialism not only leaves the facts of *this* world intact but imposes no constraints at all on possible other worlds or unwordly domains. The thesis, then, in the most fundamental respect is *useless* when properly understood.

But it is the failure to understand properly that creates what must be called artificial or bogus concerns. We can leave the "robot" thesis for a moment and consider the odd literature that has grown up around the possibility of *cloning* human beings. Any number of professional ethicists have begun to make names for themselves by asking whether clones have rights, whether they can be used for organ transplants and "farmed" for that purpose, whether they can enter into contracts, and so forth.

Perhaps it has yet to dawn on these scholars that the protections afforded by law for human beings do not originate in a theory regarding the biological processes by which human beings come into existence. The protections cover an entire class of entities—human beings—who qualify for coverage on the basis of certain attributes they share with the legislators. Nor are protections confined to legislator-like entities. We forbid cruelty toward animals not because animals are "like us" but because we believe that they are capable of experiencing pain and suffering. Accordingly, the protection is symmetrical with the capacity. If we could take one of Smith's cells, therefore, and proceed to nurture it to the point at which a copy or "clone" of Smith was produced, we would *by definition* have a human being who would thereupon enjoy all the safeguards available to conventionally produced human beings. Parents are not entitled to the kidneys or hearts of their children on the grounds that the parents "made" the children. Legal and moral rights inhere in beings of a certain kind and there is nothing in the *principled* foundations of law or morality that would justify exemptions according to modes of production. Certain ancient philosophers argued that all life arises from mixtures of air, earth, fire, and water; others thought that every existing thing could be reduced to an atomic level. At the time these theories were advanced there were developed laws and universally accepted moral injunctions. The point is that rights and duties are framed by rational beings and distributed according to capacities. The justificatory arguments are utterly indifferent to scientific theories or technical antics associated with reproductive biology. If Smith steals Jones's automobile he cannot rely for his defense on the claim that Jones—long before becoming the branch officer of the First National Bank—had been a single cell. We all began as modestly.

It is the same misunderstanding of the "clone" problem that gives rise to popular confusions when materialism makes its case. We might, for shorthand purposes, label the misunderstanding *the fallacy of origins,* for which the acronym FOO seems especially apt. What FOO produces is the unwarranted belief that to uncover the nascent state of something is to discover its true nature. The famous astronomer Dr. Carl Sagan, for example, has gone to some lengths to establish that our planet is only one of many harboring life; is not large or special in its origins; may be matched by millions or even billions of others. The implication—from the fact or the theory that Earth began in just the same way that everything else in the universe did—is that there is nothing unique about *today's* earth. As with the robot theory and human cloning, this theory too leaves everything where it found it. It is simply unarguable that our planet *is* unique. It is a storehouse of art and law; a launching pad for celestial navigators; the place where we live *our* lives. And *our* lives remain unique no matter how many others in the heavens may be living *their* lives. In the circumstance it matters not one fig that Earth was initially a ball of fire or gas or vapor. It matters not one fig that it was covered by glaciers and may be again. We all began—each and every one of us—as fertilized human eggs, as *zygotes.* But here we are, bloated with emotion, controversy, aspiration, and the possibility of daily renewal. Nothing about zygotes predicts all this or alters it in any way. To know that we began as cells is interesting and may be of benefit to us, since all knowledge contains the promise of benefits. But it does not change the facts of our lives as we now live these lives, nor does it alter what we have now earned the right to believe about our "nature." We are not "basically" or "fundamentally" or "at root" zygotes; we are *persons,* the most extraordinary production of all.

Perhaps in dismissing radical materialism as *useless* we seem to give it less standing than it has earned among philosophers at least since the time of Descartes. But the discussion to this point has been directed not at the philosophical merits of the case but only at the putative real-life implications. What should be clear is that life's aches and pains, joys and griefs survive any metaphysical interpretation of them. They also survive any scientific explanation of them. Smith's toothache is not likely to be changed by Smith's study of neurophysiology or by his dentist's account of tooth decay.

As an essentially metaphysical (rather than scientific) theory, radical materialism leaves the facts of life unchanged but urges us to understand these facts in a nontraditional way. What the materialist seeks is a total unification of knowledge under the umbrella of scientific explanation. The historical disunity has always been promulgated by those who have found in human *psychology* evidence of something special, something nonphysical, immaterial, *irreducibly* mental. Thus, in its various forms philosophical materialism has sought to prove either that all mental phenomena are actually caused by physical (brain) processes or that there are not really mental events at all. The robot or some facsimile is introduced as a way of demonstrating that at least in principle all these things we take to be mental can arise from a machine properly assembled and programmed. This is an argument from analogy and labors to defend the implication that two entities, displaying similar "outputs," must be the same *kind* of entities.

This, at last, is a fallacious argument. It is abundantly clear that, from the "output" characteristics of *any* system, it is not possible to establish the system's internal design features or principles of function. A neighbor and a tape recorder can both deliver the message, "happy birthday." An analysis of the sounds emanating from both may show that the "outputs" are nearly indistinguishable. Nonetheless, we know that the processes involved in the verbal utterance are entirely different from those governing the activity of the tape recorder. This example is sufficient to prove that no degree of purely *behavioral* similarity can establish the *essential* similarity of two different systems. We do not consider the mute devoid of thought, nor do we conclude that a paralyzed patient is incapable of *wanting* to do things. Cases could be multiplied without limit, all of them leading us to the recognition that observable *behavior* is not a reliable guide to comprehending the psychological dimensions of life. There is, to be sure, a rough correspondence between certain psychological states and conduct of a certain kind; between, for example, hunger and eating, anger and frowning, humor and smiling. But discipline in some instances and disease in others can totally eliminate this correspondence. In still other instances, there is simply no behavioral correlate available. What *behavior* corresponds to the *hope* that it will snow in January? The robot theory, therefore, does not gain credence as the fidelity of simulation increases. No matter how many humanlike behaviors such a device may emit, it never follows that the similar human behaviors arise from the same principles or are regulated by the same processes. Do computers "think"? Well, they "think" in much the same way that the tape recorder "says" "happy birthday," and in much the same way as an automobile breaks down from "fatigue." Because of the rough correspondence between some psychological states and some modes of behavior, we find it convenient to impute the same psychological attributes to anything displaying similar behavior. We do not really have any logical warrant to do this, but the habit is innocuous enough when exercised sparingly. There is a difference, however, between simple sloth and metaphysical incoherence. It is the latter that stands behind defenses of materialism grounded in the actual or possible behavior of robots. For from the robot's behavior *nothing* of psychological consequence follows. Indeed, even from the behavior of human beings nothing of psychological consequence would follow were it not for the psychological equipment of the human observer who *witnesses* the behavior of others. If a being lacked consciousness, thought, and emotion but had keen senses and some rudimentary way of storing prior perceptions, nothing in the witnessed behavior of beings could ever give rise to the concepts of consciousness, thought, and emotion. It is only because each of us possesses these attributes that we are able to ascribe them to other human beings.

To this extent we begin to see how vulnerable we are to the robot theory. We assign psychological characteristics to other human beings because they report feelings similar to our own and because their actions are much like our own actions when they claim to have thoughts or feelings similar to our own. Why not, then, ascribe the same psychological functions to a robot that reports having feelings and thoughts and that proceeds to act appropriately?

The answer to this question depends on the difference between what may be called direct, as opposed to circumstantial, evidence. The only unarguable claim regarding the existence of a thought or feeling is the one made by the person having the thought or feeling. He has *direct* evidence. But as an observer of others, he can only make inferences and identifications. In trying a case of murder, the jury has every reason to take into account the fact that the defendant had a strong motive to kill the deceased, but the motive here is not actual *evidence* of guilt. An eyewitness, however, who was in the room at the time the crime was committed—who actually *saw* the defendant strike the fatal blow—is in a position to provide noninferential information. We are, as it were, "eyewitnesses" to our own thoughts and feelings, whereas our assumptions about the thoughts and feelings of others are always circumstantial. The robot theory reminds us of just this difference between our *direct* awareness of our own psychological nature and our *indirect* awareness of and assumptions about the *apparently* similar nature of other human beings. It may well be that some future technology will create such high-fidelity simulations of human beings as to make it virtually impossible for a person to distinguish between the robots and bona fide persons. In this circumstance we could find ourselves treating these devices the same way we treat fellow humans. But there is all the difference between being gulled by a good simulation and *being* a simulation. We always have the right to think of every entity external to ourselves as a simulation, but no person thinks of *himself* that way. His psychological nature remains what it is no matter how artfully his (mere) behavior may be mimicked or copied. A good impersonator raises no doubts about the real existence of the person he is impersonating. And the person impersonated has no doubt at all about his own motives, thoughts, and feelings as he watches someone else copy his mannerisms.

Materialism's other gambit—the robots having failed—is simply to deny that there are mental states at all. This is not easy to maintain in public, but it is a thesis seriously argued in the protected duchies of academic philosophy and psychology. Let us examine in a nontechnical way how professional philosophers and psychologists think up the notion that there are no thoughts, come to believe that there are no beliefs, and feel strongly that there are no feelings.

This surprising achievement proceeds along two different and ultimately incompatible lines of argument. The first is relatively

modest but is doomed. It centers on the claim that every psychological event or state is completely and uniquely determined by the physiology of the nervous system and, more specifically, by events in the
brain. The nineteenth century dubbed this thesis *epiphenomenalism,*
and its defenders have looked to it as a means of bringing the mind
under the same laws as those governing the rest of nature. What
dooms epiphenomenalism is that it must accept the existence of mental states and events, even as it seeks to explain them. But if there are
bona fide *mental* events—events that are not themselves physical or
material—then the whole program of philosophical materialism collapses. The universe is no longer composed of "matter and a void"
but now must make (spaceless) room for (massless) entities. And as
the universe attempts to do this, the epiphenomenalist must set
himself the task of accounting for the alleged ability of matter to *cause*
these immaterial, spaceless happenings.

There is an escape clause available here: The epiphenomenalist
might argue that he is not claiming that the material brain *causes* mental events but that it is the necessary *condition* for such events. If all
that is meant by this is that the brain is needed for thought the way
Michaelangelo needed hands to forge his "David," very few "men-
talists" would voice objections. Most would say that for the mind to
realize its objectives it must do so through the material body, that it
uses the brain as a mediating device. Without a brain the mind would
not have an effective means (a necessary condition) by which to accomplish various goals. But if "necessary condition" means more
than this—if it means that the brain *must* exist and function in specific
ways *in order that there be mind*—then the epiphenomenalist not only has
not made his case but *cannot* make his case. This is so for the following
reason. On the epiphenomenalist's assumption, there are two entities
—the mental and the material—having real existence. Furthermore,
the former is alleged to be caused by the latter, in just the way that entirely material causes result in entirely material effects. But note that
in any purely physical interaction, it is never *necessary* that event A
cause event B; it is merely contingently the case, given the composition and laws of the physical world, that events of type A happen to
cause or faithfully lead to events of type B. Accordingly, to argue that
brain states, in a natural-causal fashion, produce mental states is to
admit that it could be otherwise. *All purely natural phenomena could be
other than they are.* Thus, the epiphenomenalist, to the extent that he
endorses a causal theory of brain–mind relationships, can never establish that the brain is *necessary* in order that there be mind. There is

nothing logically contradictory in the claim that there are minds without brains and brains without minds. One might argue that this is factually not so, but one cannot argue that it is *necessarily* not so. Once it is granted that there are genuinely mental (nonphysical) events, it follows that an exhaustive inventory of the *physical* universe and its laws must be incomplete as an inventory of real existents, because mental events are left out. If there can be mind in addition to matter, there can be mind without matter. The traditional argument against this thesis is that immaterial entities (if such there are) cannot have effects. But the "effects" embraced by this argument are *physical* effects. One can counter the argument merely by claiming that immaterial entities do have effects *on other immaterial entities*. And one might illustrate this by noting the effect one idea has on another in a stream of ideas.

The epiphenomenalist's causal theory should not be confused with the ordinary causal laws of the physical sciences. The latter are confined to the manner in which force and matter are distributed in time and space. But with epiphenomenalism we are faced with a radically different entity—a *mental* entity—taken to be nonmaterial and nonphysical. If it exists at all, then by definition it cannot be composed of or reduced to material elements or combinations thereof. To say that it "arises" from these is, alas, gibberish.

For these and many kindred reasons, an influential group of materialists have chosen valor over discretion and have bluntly denied that there are mental events at all. This is the school of so-called eliminative materialism, whose curriculum is designed to show that our ageless talk about minds, thoughts, feelings, and the like is but a vestige of religiomagical ignorances. It is finally "ghost talk," whose vocabulary will be properly translated by the findings of science, and thereupon eliminated from philosophically polite discourse.

As we made clear earlier in this chapter, success in a venture of this sort can only be nugatory since the psychological properties of our lives will survive any of the recipes cooked up by the metaphysicians. What could change with a triumphant materialism of this kind is the way we *talk* about such properties and the implications we draw from them. But since a rose by any other name, including a neurophysiological name, smells as sweet, we need consider only the implications and not the possibility of changes in our vocabularies.

The advertised implication is that, through a successful eliminative materialism, the mind will be absorbed completely into the natural sciences, and we will no longer labor under the mentalistic superstitions of the ages. We will finally understand that the only thing unique about us is our material organization. Equipped with this great truth we will content ourselves to live this, the only life we have. All religions will finally be seen as the mythologies they are, and, apart from literary purposes, we will speak of the "human condition" in the precise and morally neutral language of physiology. Once we understand that *everything* of psychological consequence is merely a reflection of the same sort of brain processes, we will abandon all corollaries of "demon" talk: Minds, thoughts, souls, consciousness, genius, art, and so on. If such words actually refer to anything, they refer to events in the brain.

Thus, we meet the same old robots—ourselves—now being told by other robots how misled we have been by still other robots! We do not *really* have free will, we only *think* we do; but we really don't have thoughts, either, we only *think* we do. We are inclined to believe in God because of our habit of making causal inferences when we perceive signs of design, rationality, and moral awareness. But there really is no belief, no inference, no perception, no reason, no morality, and no awareness, for these are all only brain processes.

What is new about this nonsense is not the seriousness with which it is proposed but the willingness of otherwise sensible men and women to accept it. So put off by a version of it in the eighteenth century was the philosopher George Berkeley that he developed a completely consistent *immaterialism* to put an end to it. Berkeley argued (correctly) that it would be a manifest contradiction to claim to know that of which we have no idea. In other words, every knowledge claim must be a claim about something in the mind—a perception, an image, a thought, a memory—in short, an *idea*. But an idea can only be like another idea, never like a material object. When we think of a chair, for example, our minds are not invaded by actual chairs. Thus, to know *anything* is no more than and no different from having ideas of a certain kind. Accordingly, the only consistent and noncontradictory metaphysics is one that takes only *ideas* as having real existence. Those entities we recognize as filling the material universe—chairs, stars, brains—do not and cannot exist independently of a knowing mind; rather, they *subsist* in the minds that have ideas of them. We might say that Berkeley reversed the tables on the materialists. He argued that, far from the material stuff (such as brains) being a necessary condition for mind, it is mind that is the necessary condition for there to be (subsistent) matter. His *immaterialism* was designed not to make us skeptical about the "real world" but to show us how such a world is literally and factually unimaginable in the absence of mind.

When the modern defender of materialism is offered the Berkeleyan alternative, he is likely to chortle, dismissing the argument as "solipsism" or "idealism" or simply "rubbish." These are not, of course, proofs against the argument, merely expressions of incredulity and impatience. When pressed to justify each, he is likely to turn to claims of this sort: "I can place an electrode in Smith's brain, apply a weak shock, and Smith will report seeing a flash of light or the sound of a click or an itch on his forearm. Clearly, it is the brain event that causes the mental outcome, and not *vice versa*."

But the orthodox Berkeleyan is not likely to quail in the face of this sort of demonstration. All the materialist has done here is offer a set of *perceptions* connected by the purely mental operations of inference, observation, and belief. The entire scene is enacted on the screen of the *mind,* and the allegedly material events owe their entire existence to this fact. We do not settle the dispute between Berkeley and the materialist by hurling epithets at Berkeley. In the final analysis we retreat from Berkeley's metaphysics not because it has been proved false or fallacious but because it does not satisfy our deepest intuitive understandings of the relationship between ourselves and the world around us. The materialist himself is most likely to come around to this mode of criticism, insisting that the dictates of common sense are sufficient to make us skeptical of immaterialism. And it is in this rejoinder that we find the only grounds we need to justify a similar skepticism toward eliminative materialism. A metaphysics that obliges us to deny the existence of thoughts, feelings, motives, will, memory, imagination, moral sensibility, and consciousness is false *because* it is incredible. For it to be incredible, there must be disbelief and, therefore, belief.

What should be clear from all this is that arguments seeking to reduce mind to matter or to eliminate it altogether are self-defeating precisely because they are *arguments*. All the evidence accumulating over the past centuries leaves little doubt but that the brain is a necessary condition for the expression of those signs and actions by which we recognize mind in another. It is to the lasting credit of those neuroscientists, past and present, that they have developed the methods by which these relationships between brain and mind may be studied and measured. It is important to stress, therefore, that a critique of *philosophical materialism* is not a criticism of neurobiology. The former is an utterly speculative presumption whose validity *cannot* be established scientifically and whose plausibility is wrecked by the very appeals it makes for endorsement.

If radical materialistic determinism is the counterfeit of the neural sciences, much that comes today from the specialty of "sociobiology" is the counterfeit of evolutionary biology. The radical materialist would dismiss mind either as a fiction or as the helpless and passive by-product of physiological processes. The sociobiologist—at least the reckless one—would depreciate the highest human sensibilities and institutions by taking them to be no more than evolved versions of habits found throughout the animal economy. Let us turn now to this other scientistic enterprise to note how richly it shares the fatal defects of all reductionistic programs.

Suggested Readings

BORST, C. V. (Ed.). *The mind/brain identity theory.* New York: St. Martin's Press, 1970.

LUCE, A. A. *Berkeley's immaterialism.* New York: Russell & Russell, 1968.

PUTNAM, H. Brains and behavior. In R. J. Butler (Ed.), *Analytical philosophy.* New York: Barnes & Noble, 1965.

ROBINSON, D. N. *The enlightened machine.* New York: Columbia University Press, 1980.

YOUNG, R. M. *Mind, brain and adaptation in the nineteenth century.* Oxford: Clarendon Press, 1970.

5

Moral Reasoning and Evolutionism

If we are to comprehend the deep misunderstandings that beset sociobiology we must first examine the nature of morality itself and the striking incompatibilities between the principles of evolutionary theory and the essential nature of moral reasoning. In this chapter we shall review and elucidate relevant aspects of moral philosophy and proceed to certain fallacious tendencies in the application of evolutionary theory to morals.

Freedoms, Rights, and Obligations

We might begin boldly with the concept of rights, those intangibles which have suffered a dangerous devaluation during recent decades of merry inflation. What does it mean to say that we have a *right?* As with all moral terms, this lends itself to a variety of construals. In his day-to-day activities, the citizen of the free world is likely to think of a right as something protected by law, as a freedom to act which all of us have a duty to honor. Forced to confine his notion of a right to a single sentence, the citizen is apt to say that a right is a legally guaranteed freedom of action that everyone is duty-bound to respect.

There is, however, a problem that quickly arises whenever we attempt to treat moral and legal terms as synonyms. We would not want to say, for example, that the Gestapo had a *right* to exterminate Jews because Nazi law permitted it. Indeed, history and daily life will turn up numerous instances of purely legal guarantees that seem to be quite removed from the notion of *rights* proper. We recognize, therefore, that it is entirely possible for a law or a given set of laws to permit that which, on a deeper understanding, nearly everyone would take to be wrong. It is just this possibility of a conflict between law and morals that prepares us to judge certain laws as unjust, immoral, and *wrong*. We would say, for example, that a law permitting the torture of animals would not make such actions right, just as a law permitting theft, murder, slavery, fraud, and so forth would not transform such activities into rightful ones.

In the same way we come to recognize the difference between legal and moral duties. We can say that Nazi law placed the citizens of Germany in 1940 under a *legal* obligation to report the whereabouts of Jews, but we would scarcely argue that these citizens had a *moral* duty to assist the authorities. What is important about this difference is not that nearly everyone notices it but that the very logic of morals requires it. It is important to see how this is the case, and we begin to see how when we examine the very idea of law. Implicit in the idea of law is the concept (and the fact) of human autonomy, since it would be pointless to legislate actions over which persons had no control. Where actions are inevitable no law is necessary, and where actions are impossible all law is nugatory. Thus, by its very nature law addresses the range of human actions within which choice is possible and productive of intended consequences. It is precisely for this reason that persons are held *responsible* and therefore punishable. But the punishments of law logically entail responsibility, which is to say *guilt*. And thus a law that sets about to punish those who are either guilty of nothing or whose actions have done no more than conform to the laws of physics stands as no more than a species of logical contradiction. To hold a man "guilty" of being a Jew, for example, is to charge him with that over which he could exercise no control or choice. To punish him for the same is likewise incoherent from a logical point of view, not to mention barbarous from a moral point of view.

It is quite the same with the institution of slavery. The law that permits persons to be enslaved—that "obliges" us to "honor" the "rights" of the slaveholder—is a law that appeals to us as autonomous beings for the purpose of denying human autonomy. Further, it attaches punishments and guilt to a class whose members are assigned on the basis of characteristics they did not choose and could not control, particularly the characteristic of racial identity.

It is neither necessary nor appropriate in the present context to argue for any particular moral maxim. It is enough to show the utter bankruptcy of that all too common expression of contemporary wisdom according to which morality is entirely relative and grounded in nothing firmer than personal feelings. The realm of morality is necessarily occupied by *rational* beings who give reasons for their judgments and require others to do likewise. It is an essentially *propositional* realm regulated by the universal modes of logical analysis. Its contents are confined to a small set of major premises that must be accepted as the very conditions of civilized life. The premises, once granted, lead inevitably to conclusions made necessary by logic itself and entirely immune to the caprice of sentiment, opinion, and taste. If morality did not have these attributes, it would be incoherent for the relativists to claim the sorts of "rights" allegedly sanctioned by relativism itself. From the mere *fact* that society is "pluralistic" nothing of moral consequence would follow. It surely would not be incumbent on a government or a community to "honor" the pluralism or to accord it possibilities for free expression. It could not be *unjust* to persecute dissenters or imprison those who annoy the majority. It could not be *unfair* to exploit the ignorant and weak, nor could it be *perverse* to practice genocide or infanticide. The concepts of injustice, unfairness, and perverseness—like the obligations to honor, to respect and to permit—are intelligible only within a *moral* context and to moral beings. In the mindless universe of mere nature—the universe without rational beings—there is neither justice nor mercy, neither liberty nor fairness. There are only facts, and no fact—as a fact—seeks or requires a justification.

Those who defend moral relativism are usually found not only asserting the "rights" of persons to do all sorts of things but insisting that others have a *duty* to honor these *rights*. How anyone can argue this way with a straight face is a question for experts in human intelligence and personality. But it is not necessary for us to keep a straight face while the spectacle unfolds. To have a duty to honor rights requires minimally that there are duties and rights. Since no such entities are properties of mere matter, they cannot be understood by the laws of physics. They arise, as we have shown, from the "laws of logic," as it were, and from beings who provide and expect justifications for actions of a certain kind. They come about, then, through the processes of rational discourse and not from a kind of indigestion. Whether the institution of slavery, for example, is right or wrong cannot be settled by asking citizens how they "feel" about it. If it is morally wrong, it was as wrong before the Thirteenth Amendment as it was after; as wrong in Louisianna as it is in Madrid; as wrong in 1350 as it was in 1850 or would be in 2050; as wrong for tribes that enjoy it as for tribes that forbid it; as wrong for the Hindu as it is for the Christian. There have been many, of course, who have not thought of slavery as wrong, just as there have been many who have thought incorrectly on all sorts of issues. But once it is understood that slavery can proceed only on the assumption that human beings are property—objects to be used for the pleasure or benefit of other human beings—it *necessarily* follows that no freedom of any kind can ever be defended on grounds other than the grounds of raw physical power. What slavery allows, by its very justificatory language, is the denial of the very principles on which property itself can be accorded the status of a *just possession.* As Hadley Arkes has noted, if slavery isn't wrong nothing *can* be wrong. Moreover, and to make the same point again, we do not arrive at this understanding by checking our pulse or heartbeats or intestines. This is the gift of *reason,* whose rules pervade every culture, every tribe, every grouping of rational beings, which is to say *human persons.*

What is established by all this is the *rationality* of morals and the fact that morality proper is available only to rational beings. This is to say not that all rational beings are necessarily moral but that all moral beings are necessarily rational. A purely emotional or sentimental being might be impelled toward actions that moral beings would describe as good or virtuous; but the purely emotional or sentimental being, not knowing the *reasons* behind these actions, could not be said to be moral himself. For to be impelled by emotion is to act under duress and thus to have one's actions *determined* by literally mindless forces. It is to be a slave of sorts and therefore to be irresponsible because unfree. Accordingly, today's rather common and coarse popular theory of morality—the theory that would ground morality in no more than the feelings persons have about this or that—is utterly incoherent.

But why, then, does the average person approve or condemn certain actions on the grounds of the "feelings" such actions excite? Why, that is, do we find today's witness given to such expressions as, "Well, I feel that it is wrong" or "I feel people should do this and not that"? Even more paradoxically, why has the modern world come to regard being "judgmental" as somehow unattractive and suspect?

We can begin to approach these questions by noting the strange meanings that have come to be associated with the idea of freedom. It seems to be part of today's folk philosophy to regard freedom exclusively in political and social terms, so that everyone "in a free country" is thought to be free to do anything not specifically forbidden by law. Added onto this peculiar notion is the belief that when a large enough segment of society no longer chooses to be constrained, the law in question is to be suitably modified by the political process. The popular view, then, has stripped freedom of all its moral attributes, leaving it as a mere naked social convention, which, at the political level, is a "policy." But if in fact this is all freedom is, then no one can claim it as a *right,* for rights are irreducibly moral.

Once we lose sight of the irreducibly moral character of rights, it is easy to be lulled by such reassuring maxims as those of libertarianism. It is from these that we learn, for example, that everyone has the right to do whatever he chooses so long as his actions do not deny others their rights. According to this slogan nothing is wrong as such, for each person is his own moral judge. But if nothing is wrong as such, then on what grounds can we be said to have an *obligation* to honor the rights of others? Why shouldn't the majority deny rights to the minority? If liberty itself is not morally defensible—if it can be no more than a set of conventions and policies—why should we not suspend it in our attempts to secure still other goals and social objectives?

As mere slogans neither libertarianism nor "individualism" has any redeeming social value. Traditional libertarians in the patrimony of John Stuart Mill sought to defend individualism on *utilitarian* grounds, arguing that the lonely individual may possess an ultimately useful truth of which the balance of humanity is totally ignorant; that the majority may be wrong in its reasonings and its facts; that power *per se* can never justify repression and that repression does harm in the long run; that the ultimate test of the rightness or wrongness of an action or policy is the *good on the whole* it achieves for those who are affected by it. But even if all this were correct, we could only say that it is more prudent or ''cost-effective'' to tolerate individuals, not that it is *morally* obligatory. And we could go on to declare that, since prudence itself is not *morally* obligatory, we shall decide to forgo whatever benefits individualism might produce. Besides, even if a policy has damaging consequences in the long run, why should *we* care, since *we* have no (moral) obligation to the future and no (moral) debt to the past?

Utilitarianism is so hopelessly defective that one is hard-pressed to find a point of entry for serious criticism. The utilitarian would confine all ''moral'' discourse to discourse about what is *useful* to humanity on the whole. Often utility is treated as that which is productive of happiness or that which reduces misery and unhappiness. But, of course, the truth itself can create much misery. In any event, it surely cannot be proved that TRUTH invariably yields higher rates of pleasure. Thus, in principle the utilitarian must be prepared to abandon truth on any showing that it will yield greater grief than joy. Here, then, we have a ''philosophy'' that must be *officially uncommitted to truth,* per se. How odd!

Then there is the notorious utilitarian ''calculus,'' which would seem to permit some measure of unjust misery to be imposed on a small and innocent minority as long as it can be shown that the *net* increase in human happiness is thereby maximized. (Presumably, this calculus would be indifferent to the extermination of all utilitarians if their eradication could be shown to have this maximizing result.) But even with this all set aside, we still have the spectacle of an *ism* appealing to us and instructing us in how we *ought* to treat individuals—and doing so while at the same time refusing to admit the fact of moral absolutes. The appeal can never rise higher than the level of mawkishness or cunning. We are asked (obliged?) to suffer the fool on the *possibility* that his nonsense will one day improve our collective lot. The promise is guaranteed by no more than the historical fact that some judged as fools in the past actually were cleverer than their accusers. *But most fools were not!* Thus, as a ''maximin'' calculus, utilitarianism lacks even the historical record that might give it statistical plausibility. That it has no moral plausibility is guaranteed by its own nonmoral reasoning. But where it is perhaps most deficient is in the realm of psychological plausibility, for it is abundantly clear that tolerance does not proceed from a calculation as to how an offensive person might make a long-term contribution to our happiness.

The problem of libertarianism, at least as it is defended nowadays, is that it is simply declared rather than *justified*. To give justifications for it, and for the individualism that it seeks to honor, is, alas, to find the proper set of moral axioms and logical connectives such that liberty stands as a necessity rather than a shibboleth. Unless we blind ourselves with a specious metaphysics, the search is neither long nor winding. We start—and we end—with the fact that all law, all liberty, all rights are intelligible only on the assumption that *persons are moral beings who can be bound by conscience and rational beings able to recognize the universal reach of moral imperatives*. What confers liberty on the individual is not something mysterious about individuals but the *universal* reach of certain moral prohibitions. If it were the individual's mere individuality that established rights we would not be justified in opposing him even in self-defense. The prohibition against murder arises not from a superstitious conviction that persons possess occult or sacred properties but from the *rational* bond that connects law, responsibility, guilt, and punishment. To ask if we have a "right" to kill Smith is to appeal to the language of justifications, which is finally an appeal to a set of moral propositions. These very propositions imply that persons have sufficient autonomy to perform certain intended actions and therefore to be responsible for them. Thus, we have a "right" to behave toward Smith in a manner that is consistent with the very nature of rights. We have a right, for example, to prevent Smith from doing the sorts of things that are destructive of rights themselves. Put in the simplest terms, we have a right to prevent what is wrong and, by the same logic, we have no "right" to do what is wrong. Libertarianism does have a moral foundation, and one quite a bit sturdier than anything utilitarian ethics can provide. Its foundation is the human capacity to be responsible for one's actions and never to be obliged by the law to do that which contradicts the very terms on which law itself comes into being.

In this all too hurried exploration of the nature of rights and moral reasoning, we have aimed only at noting the irreducibly rational—the formal, propositional—character of moral discourse. Now let us proceed to that brand of modern evolutionism that would seek to explain all this in utterly naturalistic and "value-free" terms. As will become clear, our target is not evolutionary *biology* or evolutionary science, but the dogmatic *evolutionism* that now enjoys such wide attention.

Evolutionism and the Fallacy of Origins

This is not an easy time to write against the theory of evolution because of the strong possibility of guilt by association. We hear much these days about something called "Creation Science," which takes as one of its fundamental tenets the accuracy of the Book of Genesis as a technical account of the formation of the universe. We would hope it would not be necessary to dissociate ourselves from this perspective. But since we do live in suspicious times, times in which journalists choose headline-hunting over honest labor, let us make our position clear on the theory of evolution: WE CAN FIND NO EVIDENCE TO DISCONFIRM, AND WE ACKNOWLEDGE OVERWHELMING EVIDENCE TENDING TO SUPPORT, THE GENERAL PRINCIPLES DEVELOPED BY DARWIN AND SUBSEQUENTLY REFINED BY THE SCIENTIFIC COMMUNITY, TO ACCOUNT FOR THE ANATOMICAL DIVERSITY OF THE PLANT AND ANIMAL KINGDOMS. This is not to say that Darwinian and neo-Darwinian formulations are free of all difficulties. There is some evidence accumulating to the effect that the *gradual* evolution of new forms is not the main mode of evolution, but that quite abrupt transitions (mutations) occurred, and that these are, in fact, the source of gradual evolution itself. Moreover, reading fossil records is part art and part science, and it may be that a now unforeseen reading will result in evolutionary formulations quite unlike those now widely accepted by competent scientists. This is not the place to weigh these possibilities, however, so we must content ourselves and the reader with merely recording our principled willingness to abide by the best available scientific reckonings. These, as it happens, are essentially Darwinian, improved by a genetic science that was unavailable to Darwin and his contemporaries.

But the problem is not with Darwin's biology, it is with his *psychology* and with the manner by which this ill-conceived psychology has now been made "official" by the sociobiologists. The first edition of *Origin of Species* appeared in 1859, when Darwin was already a celebrated naturalist, and nearly a century after evolutionary thinking had pretty much become standard fare within the international

scientific community. Nearly all the famous "progressive" philosophers of the eighteenth-century Enlightenment subscribed to an
evolutionary theory of social and economic history, some of them going so far as to propose processes that, by a variety of names, were all
akin to the laws of *natural selection* and the principle of *survival of the fit-
test.* The eighteenth century's *idea of progress* became the Victorians'
religion of progress, both grounded in the thesis that history is organic
and natural and that it is only through free competition that the best
"forms"—whether economic, artistic, or personal—are created.

Part of our contemporary folklore includes the picture of a
maligned and misunderstood Darwin, the victim of petty orthodoxy
and smug know-nothingism, supported by a tiny band of brave truth-
seekers persecuted as Galileos in Victorian dress. Well, yes and no,
but mostly no. The major journals of the day greeted *Origin of Species*
with a respect bordering on reverence. Combined, the *London Review,*
the *Edinburgh Review,* and the *Dublin Review* devoted more than a hundred pages to appraisals of the book. The author was uniformly
praised for his previous accomplishments and for that genius for
observation so evident in this, his most important contribution to
date. One reviewer regretted that this extraordinary work should be
marred by a "horrid genealogy," and others remarked that no one
ever doubted that man is an animal—though not *merely* an animal—
but on the whole the reviews were fair, laudatory, searching. Very
nearly every criticism was framed in the best scientific evidence
available at the time. More than one critic challenged Darwin's claim
that the theory suffers from the incompleteness of the fossil record.
The record, they noted, was *too good,* and tended to disconfirm a
theory proposing gradual evolution and the production of entirely
new species. What the record did disclose were the very discrete
species embodied in older views of "special creation." Still other
critics observed that, after centuries of domestic breeding, no species
ever became something other than what it started as. Thus, while
praising Darwin for his unprecedented rigor of observation and
recording, the major reviews left room for the possibility that the
story was not quite the whole story, and that its theoretical linchpin
might actually be defective. None of the principal reviewers was
dismissive or depreciating; none cried "heresy"; none was startled or
aghast. More than one local parson would cry out against such blas-
phemy and would seek to preserve the literal truth of scripture, but
Darwin was scarcely alone as a target of fundamentalist rebuke. In

the circles that counted he and his thick book were greeted with
cautious admiration.

However, in the decade following *Origin of Species* the *theory* of
evolution quickly took on the colors of a movement, Darwinism,
whose cardinal beliefs would be set forth in a very different book, *The
Descent of Man* (1871). In this work Darwin was not the disinterested
naturalist, the compulsive recorder of fact, the reluctant theorist.
Rather, he surfaces as the champion of an idea, arguing that the full
range of human *psychological* and *moral* characteristics arise from and
are patterned after characteristics found abundantly in the animal
kingdom. Not only do the great apes anticipate our anatomical and
physiological attributes, but they prove their shared ancestry by
displaying the emotional, social, and intellectual features thought to
be uniquely human. The same case is forcefully repeated in his *The
Expression of the Emotions in Man and Animals* (1872). It was in these
works and in the polemical defenses of them by Darwin's supporters
(chiefly Thomas Henry Huxley) that the war between science and religion was declared. Bishop Wilberforce, presiding at Oxford,
asked whether his ape-pedigree was to be found on his maternal or
paternal side, giving Huxley the debater's luxury of standing on the
side of modest truth. In his reply to the Bishop Huxley won over the
Oxford audience by admitting that he would rather claim an ape for a
relative than a man who refused to use his reason and judgment in
weighing evidence and reaching just conclusions. On a different oc-
casion at the same university Benjamin Disraeli distilled the controversy to its essence: whether we are apes by another name or are
just below the angels. For his part, Disraeli chose to stand "on the
side of the angels."

Before the nineteenth century ended there would be a rash of
psychological texts all pretty much taking the Darwinian thesis for
granted. Psychology was at the time (as it has been since) eager to
establish its scientific credentials, and science in this dispute was
almost entirely with the Darwinians. Hoping to secure scientific
status for their discipline, the new psychologists attempted to move
the traditional problems of psychology into laboratories, where, it
was thought, the mere act of measuring would eliminate all ambi-
guity and settle all controversy. In one of those accidents that are so
productive of irony, the psychology laboratory proved to be especially
inhospitable to the phenomena of abstract reasoning, language, and
ethics, though well suited to the study of elementary sensory processes and rudimentary forms of learning and memory. These latter

functions are, of course, just the ones abundantly present among all advanced species. Accordingly, nothing arising from the experimental observations of animals challenged the contention that all of human psychology is to be explained in evolutionary terms. In selecting precisely those processes that are known to be nearly universally distributed among the higher species, the experimental psychologists virtually guaranteed support for a Darwinian psychology. When it came to such hard cases as human language, abstract reasoning, or moral concern, this new *scientistic* psychology offered soothing reassurances, some of them provably false, e.g. that the chimpanzee lacks the necessary vocal anatomy to speak; that "abstract" reasoning is simply a chain of trial-and-error "associations"; that mankind's alleged morality is found in the altruistic, maternal, and social tendencies displayed by many animals and all primates.

It would be perhaps harsh to declare that nothing of a substantive nature has validated this perspective in the century since its inauguration. The theory—let us call it "psychological Darwinism"— could not handle hard cases then and cannot handle them now. With respect to language, for example, the only additions to the older naturalistic observations have been experiments on the learning of "sign language" by monkeys and chimpanzees, as described in Chapter 8. Extravagant claims have been made by many, but the fairest account is that what has been learned by these animals is but a chain of responses, each element of which has become associated with a specific object or a discrete action: "Bob—give—Lana— orange." There seems to be nothing in such chains that would prevent pigeons or rats from acquiring the same sequences. What is conspicuously absent is any evidence of a comprehension of the *connotations* of words or signs. The animals can use those symbols that *denote* specific movements ("give") and objects ("Bob"), but none that *connotes* abstract meanings. That is, we have no evidence of the intelligent combination of elements of the sort, "Bob—give—Lana— justice"!

It is not to be thought that all this will somehow be settled "in a matter of time," for what is problematic here is not the techniques of training or measuring but the literal impossibility of proving, from the responses of animals to various stimuli, the presence of a comprehension of the abstract meaning of these stimuli. It is one thing to train an animal to stop moving when a octagonal sign is displayed or when we say "Halt!" It is quite another, however, to jump from this fact to the conclusion that the animal is aware of an *obligation* to *obey* the *commands* issued by a *constitutionally empowered* authority. If all one means by "language" is a string of symbols or stimuli capable of initiating specific responses on the part of an observer, then cloud formations are "telling" us of forthcoming rain and the noise from the chicken coop is intended to alert us to the proximity of a fox. But the term *language* connotes far more than this. It refers not only to law-governed sequences of symbolic expression but also to the symbolic representation of complex and abstract *concepts* for which there is no objective or material equivalent. This is at least what human language has always included, even when expressed in the most primitive cultures or the most remote ages. It is what we *mean* by language, and it is precisely because of this that dolphins, chimpanzees, "lovebirds," and the rest just don't qualify. All of the advanced species are able to form complex behavioral chains, including chains of vocalization, in an attempt to secure rewards or avoid punishments from the environment. There is no harm done to logic or to the facts of the case by saying that our dogs are "loyal," that our kittens are "playful," or that robins are "good mothers." If what we mean by *loyalty* is the tendency of an animal to endure pain and hardship in order to remain close to its master—the tendency to do even self-harming things on the command of its master—then surely dogs have compiled an exceptional record of loyalty. The damage is done, however, when we insist on treating the *dog's* form of loyalty as indistinguishable from human loyalties, where we know the latter are grounded in *principles* of obligation and where the former provides no evidence of the same. It may well be man's fate to have to rationalize those virtues which our pets practice by nature, but so be it. There are, to be sure, many contexts in which human obedience and the human fulfillment of duties are based on factors practically identical to those governing the behavior of animals. But there are too many exceptions to this, and it makes no sense, in the name of "scientific objectivity," to ignore or deny them. We can praise and love animals for their instinctive and noble sentiments without confusing these with the reasoned and vexatious analyses that form the essential ingredient in all significant human relationships.

The issue here is not whether monkeys or cats or dogs "reason," for stated this way any reply will find some basis in fact. What we do know about *human* reasoning is that it is capable of framing universal propositions in such a way as to arrive at universally true conclusions. There is simply not a shred of evidence to suggest that any nonhuman animals do likewise. It is not something they do less well, but something they do not at all. A man can know he is guilty but may be utterly remorseless. The dog's guilt is just this *feeling,* with nothing universal superadded. The saint and the hero do what they do in the interest of principles and abstractions that dictate which is "right" regardless of consequences. We can say that a dog has performed "heroically" without confusing its behavior with the saint's or the hero's. To confuse the two is to beg the very question of evolutionary theory, not to answer it. This theory in every form, from the pen of Darwin and under all its later revisions, is either limited to the anatomical and physiological variations of nature or, in addition to these, includes human psychology as well. If *psychological Darwinism* is to be assessed as a theory, we are not entitled to take its truth for granted. Rather, we must array all the known aspects of human psychology against it and summon its defenders to show how the theory is able to explain them.

The *facts* of human morality and ethics are clearly at variance with a theory that explains all behavior in terms of self-preservation and the preservation of the species. It is frighteningly conceivable that the human race will risk its own total annihilation over the very *principles* on which human life is to be governed and lived. This may be judged unsound, but its possibility is enough to suggest that "natural selection" has not fashioned an ethics of this sort. Nor is it at all clear how "natural selection" has somehow selected for Bach's Partitas or for abstract geometries that can be true of no possible world or for a system of justice that will let a thousand guilty men go free lest one innocent man be constrained of his liberties. We do not legislate here the final standing of Darwinism. We note only that there is no version of it able to address these facts of human life and that, accordingly, we are obliged by the dictates of reason to accept the profound (even if temporary) limitations of the theory.

Let us now narrow our focus and examine contemporary sociobiology, the offshoot of evolutionary theory, the hybrid discipline that seeks to understand the most complex social phenomena according to the principles of evolutionary biology.

Selected Readings

ARKES, H. *The philosopher in the city: The moral dimensions of urban politics.* Princeton, N. J.: Princeton University Press, 1981.

BOCK, K. E. *Human nature and history*. New York: Columbia University Press, 1980.

FINNIS, J. *Natural law and natural rights*. Oxford: Clarendon Press, 1980.

ROBINSON, D. N. *Psychology and law: Can justice survive the social sciences?* New York: Oxford University Press, 1980.

6

The Human Person
in Society

Society has developed in cultural evolution from the primitive basis of an irrational or instinctive association of human beings to a highly organized structure governed by values. As indicated in Figure 6-1 biological evolution has created the human genotypes that build human brains with propensities for altruistic behavior and all other cultural activities, which would include the value systems molding and governing society. Values are important constituents of World 3, being included under philosophy in Figure 3-3.

The Origin of Values

Values can be thought of very simply as what we value. They are at the basis of our judgments and our choices: whether to do this or that. Each of us has a scale of values or a value system that may not be consciously recognized but which, nevertheless, provides a framework

EVOLUTION

BIOLOGICAL EVOLUTION OF GENOTYPES	CULTURAL EVOLUTION, HUMAN EXCLUSIVELY
Phenotypes Built by Genotypes	
Animal Brain with Pseudaltruistic Behavior	
Human Brain With Propensity for Language	Learning of Specific Human Languages
Human Brain with Propensity for Altruistic Behavior	Learning of Altruistic Behavior
Human Brain with Propensity for All Cultural Performances	Learning of Culture

FIGURE 6-1. General Diagram of Evolution. The vertical line effects a sharp separation between biological evolution and cultural evolution. To the left are entirely World 1 objects: genotypes, phenotypes, animal brains, and human brains. By contrast, to the right are exclusively World 3 objects: language, values, and all of culture as indicated in Figure 3-3.

for our decisions. But, of course, its role is to condition, not to determine. Such rules of conduct are just as much learned as is language. As stated in Chapter 8, the brain is built with a propensity for language. Great linguistic areas of the neocortex have been developed in biological evolution and are at birth preformed before being used for whatever language is heard. So also the brain is built with the propensity for performance according to value systems, and the value system initially learned is that of the ambient culture.

Just as there are rudimentary animal communications (Chapter 8), so there are rudimentary social organizations in which behavior patterns have both an instinctive and a learned basis. Presumably this "society" of our primate forebears formed the basis from which there developed the "culture" of early hominids. We can conjecture that the motivation was the need for social cohesion in organized hunting and warfare, in food-sharing, and in the development of tool manufacture. For example, there is the actual record of the very gradual development of the hand ax over hundreds of thousands of years. But most important would be the gradual improvement in linguistic communication to give social cohesion.

As Sherrington in his Gifford Lectures reviews the evolutionary origin of man, he writes most vividly:

We think back with repugnance to that ancient biological prehuman scene whence, so we have learned, we came; there *no* life was a sacred thing. For man, largely emancipated from those conditions, the situation has changed. . . . The change is in himself. Where have his "values" come from? Those other creatures than himself, even the likest to himself, would seem without the values. There arises for him a dilemma and a contradiction. The contradiction is that he is slowly drawing from life the inference that altruism, charity, is a duty incumbent upon thinking life. That an aim of conscious conduct must be the unselfish life. But that is to disapprove the very means which brought him hither, and maintains him. Of all his new-found values perhaps altruism will be the most hard to grow. The "self" has been so long devoted to itself as end. Man is grappling with its newly found "values," yet with no experience except its own, no counsel but its own.

Already in the first great civilization, the Sumerian, there had been the earliest document of human rights, the Code of Ur-Nammu at about 2100 B.C., and also superb artistic, literary, and technological developments. Presiding over the complex creative society of a Sumerian city-state with their code of values was the priestly bureaucracy of the Ziggurat, deriving its authority from the god or system of gods whose deliverances were interpreted by the priests into rules of conduct for the affairs of the people of the state. It has recently been proposed by Julian Jaynes that the priests of the Ziggurat were not charlatans but that, when in hallucinatory trances, they heard voices which they genuinely believed to be the voices of the god!

In retrospect we can recognize that the societies of the early civilizations were governed by systems of values that were prescriptions of conduct and of judgment. Moreover these systems were slowly evolving and, just as today, were very different for the different cultures—Sumerian, Egyptian, Babylonian, Indian, Chinese.

It appears that this pervasive cultural milieu was unconsciously accepted without critical examination. The conscious recognition of values seems to have begun with Socrates, who persisted in asking new questions relating to the value of knowing; to the purposes of such activities as science, politics, and the practical arts; and even to the course of nature. These questions led to the concept that everything had a value, that is, to the general notion of value.

With this background Plato developed his ideas of essences or ideals, of which the most important were the Good, the Beautiful, and the True. They were conceived to be eternal, of divine origin, and to be the Absolutes against which all values were judged. It must be recognized that this Platonic Third World is completely different from the World 3 of Popper (cf. Figure 3–3) in that it is of divine origin, whereas the Popperian World 3 is entirely human in origin. It is also different in respect of its absolute status. According to Plato, if anything else apart from the ideal of absolute beauty is beautiful, then it is beautiful *for the sole reason* that it has some share in the ideal of absolute beauty. *And this kind of explanation applies to everything.* This idealist Trinity of Absolute Values survived in the idealist philosophies of recent times.

Values in Our Society

Werner Heisenberg has presented wise and deep statements on values in our present society:

> The problem of values is nothing but the problem of our acts, goals and morals. It concerns the compass by which we must steer our ship if we are to set a true course through life. The compass itself has been given different names by various religions and philosophies; happiness, the will of God, the meaning of life—to mention just a few. I have the clear impression that all such formulations try to express man's relatedness to a central order. . . . In the final analysis, the central order, or the "one" as it used to be called and with which we commune in the language of religion, must win out. And when people search for values, they are probably searching for the kind of actions that are in harmony with the central order, and as such are free of the confusions springing from divided, partial orders. The power of the "one" may be gathered from the very fact that we think of the orderly as the good, and of the confused and chaotic as the bad.

The great philosopher-physicist Eddington has expressed beliefs comparable with those of Heisenberg. The possibility of the arbitrariness of values derived in human consciousness led him to a belief in absolute values and that we can "trust optimistically that our values are some pale reflection of those of the Absolute Valuer."

Although the World 3 of Popper is entirely of human origin, it can approach to an absolute value. For example, Popper states with respect to the methodology of science: "Thus the elimination of error leads to the objective growth of our knowledge—of knowledge in the objective sense. It leads to the growth of objective verisimilitude; it makes possible the approximation to (absolute) truth."

Popper regards science as a *search* for absolute truth, which though unattainable is the goal and criterion of our efforts.

The great physicist Max Planck made a striking affirmation of his belief in absolute values:

> I emphasized that I had always looked upon the search for the absolute as the noblest and most worth while task of science. These absolute values in science and ethics are the ones whose pursuit constitutes the true task of every intellectually alert and active human being. This task is never finished—a fact guaranteed by the circumstance that genuine problems . . . constantly appear in ceaseless variety and constantly set new tasks for active human beings. For it is work which is the favourable wind that makes the ship of human life sail the high seas, and as for the evaluation of the worth of this work, there is an infallible, time-honoured measure, a phrase which pronounces the final authoritative judgement for all times: *By their fruits ye shall know them!*

The teaching of moral values to the young is often derided as indoctrination or even as brainwashing. Would these critics also make the same criticisms of the teaching of a language? We would maintain that it is a crime against children to leave them to their own devices in learning a language. They can suffer as a result from a lifelong verbal crippling. The wonderful genetic building of a brain for all human expressions in language is left derelict, for that is what happens if it is not intensively developed in the formative years. The same is true for moral education. The impressionable brain of the child has to be given moral instruction; otherwise that child will grow into an adult permanently maimed or flawed in human qualities. This is as much a crime as to bring children up with an inadequate linguistic performance. This is indicated in Figure 6–1 and by the ladder of personhood (Figure 3–4) for ascent to the fullest possible life.

A deficiency in moral education in the home, in the schools, and in the churches is now tragically apparent in the breakdown of the family and in the pervasive permissiveness demanded by adolescents and accorded to them. Value systems that have been built up in culture over many hundreds of years are now deteriorating so that society is threatened by newly developing barbarisms. Crime of all kinds—theft, violence, murder, kidnapping, drug-trafficking—is increasing at a menacing rate. The prison population is growing as never before. Such are the evils stemming from the failure of moral education. While there is so much public interest in the prevention of nuclear war with its threatened destruction of society from without, there is lamentably little interest in the destruction of the society from within by the failure of our system of values.

Conclusions on Values

The cultural achievements of mankind bear witness to the search for absolute values that has motivated and inspired the great creative geniuses. It can be said that, symbolically, absolute values have provided a guiding beacon. This can be appreciated when we consider the scientific efforts of Kepler, Newton, and Einstein to understand the natural world. A similar guidance of geniuses can be discerned in other fields of cultural achievement: philosophy, religion, literature, history, and the arts. The thoughts and aspirations of mankind in respect of truth, goodness, and beauty have led to the search for justice and for codes of ethics in social organization. The traditional values of truth, goodness, and beauty are intertwined in the great cultural achievements and are used as criteria of judgment. No claim should be made that absolute values have been attained in any human enterprise. Nevertheless, the quest for highest values gives the adventure of human personhood with the unsought reward of happiness in fulfillment.

Sociobiology

In the attempt to understand the complexity of the social life that has evolved in our civilization, an appealing strategy is to study animal behavior. Surely, it is argued, there must be patterns of animal behavior that, when studied dispassionately, will give insights into the motivations, ideals, urges, aggressions, ambitions, and altruisms that apparently govern the lives of individuals in our human societies.

 In his monumental treatise on sociobiology, Edward Wilson has created a new science of animal behavior that is based principally upon biological evolution and the genetic explanation of heredity. It is the claim of Wilson that the methodology and findings of sociobiology are applicable also to the social behavior of *Homo sapiens* and that his new synthesis would provide for anthropology and sociology an objective scientific basis. The strong criticisms to which Wilson was subjected were based on his premise that human behavior is genetically determined.

Sociobiology is a challenging discipline with the most fascinating stories of animal behavior. However, we cannot accept the way in which these observations on animals are used to support dogmatic statements in the field of human psychology and ethics. After the controversial reception of his first book, Wilson has followed by a book, *On Human Nature,* more specifically directed to the human situation. When Wilson leaves the field of sociobiology and embarks on dogmatic statements on ethical issues, he opens himself to criticism on moral grounds. His statements are examples of the fundamentally flawed concepts of human nature that are developed by sociobiologists whose expertise is limited to nonhuman animals, and particularly to the social insects. In criticism it can be stated that sociobiologists have misunderstood human nature because of their concentration on models of animal behavior largely derived from studies on social insects. Such behavioral terms as altruism and selfishness have been used indiscriminately for insects and for human beings. The use of the word "altruism" by sociobiologists has been at the root of our misunderstandings.

Altruism and Pseudaltruism

In the customary usage altruism is applied to the ethics of human behavior. An altruistic act is recognized by the *intention* to act in a manner designed with *regard* for the interests of other persons. Even if disastrous consequences supervene, the action still can rank as altruistic if it genuinely has the two features, *intent* and *regard.* It is evident that the ordinary social life of well-meaning persons is a tissue of altruistic actions. Selfishness is eschewed. Such altruistic actions arise on the basis of a moral education of the human person as illustrated in Figure 6–1. In contrast the "altruism' of the sociobiologists has as its exemplars the self-sacrificing behaviors particularly of the social insects. Examples are the sacrificial deaths of soldier ants, of honey bees stinging intruders, and also of birds uttering warning cries. These sacrificial actions are purely instinctive, being the consequences of the building by genetic codes of the organisms exhibiting these behaviors. They are not learned, even in the smallest degree. In order to avoid the confusions of using the same word, altruism, for superficially similar but radically different forms of behavior, we have proposed that the "altruism" of the sociobiologists be termed *pseudal-*

truism, the term *altruism* continuing to be applied in the accustomed manner to the ethics of human behavior.

What we are calling pseudaltruism would correspond to all behavior patterns that have been developed in biological evolution. With human persons they remain as the vestigial remnants of our animal ancestry. We have such vestiges in the simpler forms of linguistic communication, such as calls and cries. On the other hand, altruism develops in our cultural evolution, just as does language (cf. Figure 6–1). The *propensity to altruism* is inherited as a property of the neural machinery of the human brain, and it arose in biological evolution. Altruism is one of the glories of our human culture, and it must be learned just as we learn a language. It is no more biologically inherited than is the speaking of a particular language.

The emotionally charged conflicts over sociobiology arise because there is a dogmatic assumption that the study of animal behavior gives the key to the understanding of human behavior in every aspect. Our criticism has the aim not of discrediting sociobiology but of showing how unacceptable is its uncritical application to human sociology.

The evidence of altruistic behavior in hominids is surprisingly sparse. However, with Neanderthals 80,000 years ago we have the first known examples of ceremonial burials, which certainly are altruistic acts that can be associated with the coming of self-consciousness, with the recognition of oneself and others as conscious selves. The first evidence for compassionate behavior in human prehistory (60,000 years ago) has recently been discovered by Solecki in the skeletons of two Neanderthal men that were incapacitated by severe injuries. The bones indicated that these incapacitated creatures had been kept alive for up to two years, which could have occurred only if they had been cared for by other individuals of the tribe. Compassionate feelings can also be inferred from the remarkable discovery that burials at that time in the Shanidar cave were associated with floral tributes, as disclosed by pollen analysis. We thus may date the earliest known signs of altruism in human prehistory to 60,000 years ago. One could hope that it might be earlier, because Neanderthal men with brains as large as ours existed at least 80,000 years ago.

In his great book *Man on his Nature,* Sherrington dramatically refers to the mysterious origin of morality and thus of altruism. Mother Nature, as exhibited in biological evolution, apostrophizes man:

You are my child. Do not expect me to love you. How can I love—I who am blind necessity? I cannot love, neither can I hate. But now that I have brought forth you and your kind, remember you are a new world unto yourselves, a world which contains in virtue of you, love and hate, and reason and madness, the moral and immoral, and good and evil. It is for you to love where love can be felt. That is, to love one another.

Bethink you too that perhaps in knowing me you do but know the instrument of a Purpose, the tool of a Hand too large for your sight as now to compass. Try then to teach your sight to grow.

We have great empathy with the great master, Sherrington, in his deeply moving message. We believe that the biological evolution is not simply chance and necessity. That could never have produced us with our values. We can sense with him that evolution may be the instrument of a Purpose, lifting it beyond chance and necessity at least in the transcendence that brought forth human creatures gifted with self-consciousness. Cultural evolution then takes over from biological evolution and soon becomes crucial in natural selection, not only because of the wealth of technological innovations but also because of the creation and development of our values. For example, altruism serves well in giving the moral basis for a society dedicated to the welfare of its members.

Love and Compassion

We shall endeavor to build upon simple religious teachings that we have to love one another. If our readers have not experienced love, it is futile for us to define it or to describe it, just as it would be futile to describe color to a blind person. But, we hope, all have loved and have been loved. The deep emotional attachment between a man and a woman in love is a special example of a much more general relationship between persons. Despite the sociobiologists, loving and caring for others is still practiced. If we are fortunate we have deep feelings of empathy for our friends and relatives with no thought of any material benefits that they can bestow on us, though of course we rejoice in reciprocated love.

An ideal society would be blessed by a whole tissue of loving relationships. Persons of good will do strive to create such a society. Like the other absolute values, a society running on love is an unattainable ideal, but we can struggle toward it, particularly in a family group. It is an unforgettable experience to be immersed in the loving relationships of such a family with its transcendent happiness. This is largely the mother's achievement, with her loving care from babyhood onward as described in Chapter 2.

But this is an imperfect world, and we must be grateful for families and social groupings in which love is at least a keynote. Otherwise the ideal of love would be lost. It is important to recognize that love spreads beyond the focal group. There is a caring for others, particularly those in distress, that is based on the ability to identify with them in one's imagination, that is, in compassionate love. But in the real world of competition between power-oriented individuals love is at a minimum. It is the deplorable world that Edward Wilson writes about in his book *On Human Nature*. It is the world that is abhorred by many of the youth of today, though they wrongly identify it with its materialist evils such as pollution, armaments, and capitalist exploitation, whereas we would also emphasize communist domination.

However, in our modern world there are remarkable personal examples of altruism and compassion that are based on love. We can cite Dr. Albert Schweitzer of Lambaréné, Mother Theresa of Calcutta, and Dr. Giuseppe Maggi of the Cameroons. They have all dedicated their lives to caring for others who are in dire need of help.

There is a long and rich tradition of the history of love and its dominant role in literature—early romances, poetry, and novels. From earliest Christian times there have been two conflicting aspects of love, named Agapé, sacred or Christian love, and Eros, or pagan love with its passion and dominant erotic character. In fact, what we are writing about and what we experience in our secular lives is an intermediate between Agapé and Eros.

We should distinguish even erotic love from sex in its anatomical, physiological, and psychological manifestations, though there is a lamentable tendency toward identification of the two in these unchivalrous times. We are not denying the sexual aspect of love but merely saying that love is much more than sex. Love is a deep relationship between two human beings replete with remembrances, dedication, sacrifices, and ideals. So often in literature love is unfulfilled or lost after an ecstatic fulfillment. Then it may become a source of longing and even despair. But we may be fortunate in being able to relive and enjoy our lost love in memory and imagination. Denis de Rougement has written with deep insight and scholarship on the theme of love in his great book *Love in the Western World*. He develops the theme that the story of Tristan and Isolde has been the model of so much love literature through the centuries.

Dante tells in his "La Vita Nuova" of his transcendent love for Beatrice, a love that was never fulfilled. In reading it one feels that it is told with poetic exaggeration of feelings of a teenage Italian for a young girl. That cheap conclusion has to be confronted with the great creativity that later burst forth, *The Divine Comedy* in memory of that love, with his story of his journey, accompanied by Vergil, through the Inferno and the Purgatorio to meet the sanctified Beatrice in the Paradiso. In romantic human history love has, as in this example, transcended eroticism and often has been sublimated in great artistic creation. In his later life Michelangelo was inspired by his unfulfilled love for a wonderful person, Vittoria Colonna, a love that flowered in many love poems from each. The Lucy poems of William Wordsworth were inspired by his love for the simple country girl Lucy, who died when nine years old.

Even in the days of our youth we had years of loving, adoration, and passion with no thought of sexual gratification. Nevertheless, feelings were deep and welled over into creative thinking, far more, so, we would suspect, than in today's permissive society, when often the beginning of what could be a dedicated love is stifled by instant fulfillment. So much of today's literature and the media are oriented to pornography, yet there are still examples of dedicated love with deeply moving feelings. For example, in his great novel *The French Lieutenant's Woman* John Fowles portrays Charles Smithson as the dedicated and at the end unrequited lover of Sarah Woodruff.

It may be asked: To what category of the inner sense of Figure 3-1 does love belong? The obvious answer is: in all categories—in thoughts, feelings, memories, dreams, imaginings, intentions, and attentions.

We hope that society can recover from the trough of pornographic sex into which we have descended. We are not referring, of course, to the exposure of our bodies to the sun and the sea, but to the exhibitionism of pornography. Such exhibitions degrade our love life. We do not wish our mutual loving to be just a performance of two bodies. There is so much to be enjoyed at the spiritual level in the wonder of intimate human relationships lived in a double illumination—by the lambent light of Agapé and by the vivid light of Eros. For the mystery of love we must be eternally grateful. It can give so much joy and happiness to the adventure of human personhood.

Aggression

At the outset it is important to distinguish, as does William Thorpe, between aggression and violence. Aggressiveness is a normal biological character in the struggle for existence. Violence is an aggressive behavior definitely directed toward harming others.

There is an enormous literature on human aggression. It has become an industry! This doctrine of innate human aggression to an extreme degree has been poured out by a phalanx of writers who either have deliberately biased the evidence or have been very limited and selective in the evidence they recognize. In Ashley Montagu's book *The Nature of Human Aggression* there is a powerful attack on the extreme aspects of this doctrine of innate human aggression. One can hope that it will help to discredit the dogmas promulgated by those who believe in the intrinsic evil of mankind—almost beyond hope.

A myth promulgated by the innate aggressionists is the human preeminence among all mammals in exhibiting behavior leading to violent conflict and death. Ethologists have now reported a greater aggressiveness in several species of mammals. For example Edward Wilson states:

> On the contrary, murder is far more common and hence "normal" in many vertebrate species than in man. . . . In fact, if some imaginary Martian zoologist visiting Earth were to observe man as simply one more species over a very long period of time, he might conclude that we are among the more pacific mammals as measured by serious assaults or murders per individual per unit of time, even when our episodic wars are averaged in.

Of course, the historical record of mankind is replete with fighting and killing, but we are apt to overlook the unrecorded lives of the great bulk of the people who lived beneath all this surface of chivalric violence. The wonderful architecture from Romanesque times right through to the Renaissance is a proof of the hardworking creativity of the people despite the veneer of violence. Chaucer's *Canterbury Tales* gives a good example of humanity in the latter part of the fourteenth century. It is replete with good humor and coarseness, but not with violence.

We will now survey the case of human aggression from general principles. It is essentially the nature–nurture debate. Our brains are built with the inherited genetic instructions plus all manner of secondary influences in the developmental process. This statement can be made only as a general principle. The details are unknown. From birth onward the human being is subjected to all the environmental influences of the culture, and so comes to be a human person. The significance of the environmental influence cannot be overestimated (cf. Figure 6–1). Under the influence of a broken home environment and a sense of rejection a child can be alienated and be absorbed into groups that practice uncurbed aggression that spills over into violence.

There probably has always been some mesmeric attraction in spectacles of violence. We can read with revulsion of the Roman gladiatorial combats, which today continue in a less extreme form in such human aggressions as boxing. But today horror movies and TV crime shows are the popular attractions. As Friedrich von Hayek so well states:

> It is the harvest of those seeds that we are now gathering. Those non-domesticated savages who represent themselves as alienated from something they have never learnt . . . are the necessary product of a permissive education which fails to pass on the burden of culture, and trusts to the *natural instincts which are the instincts of the savage.*

It is a remarkable tribute to humanity that, even with such terrible indoctrination in violence, our society is so peaceful. The academic mandarins who write books on the depravity of mankind do not seem to realize the essential decency of the common people, as they would call them.

We present therefore the thesis that human beings are born with the potentiality to become fine human persons living in harmony with their fellow beings. Given a good home base and a good environment with their schoolfellows, they can be relatively untouched by the horrors of much of the so-called entertainment industry and the aggressive literature. We all inherit brains with neuronal machinery appropriate for aggressive acts just as we have neuronal machinery for linguistic acts. Speaking is dependent on learning, however, and so are aggressive behavior and violence. We can learn to control, which is the function of our great neocortex. As we have emphasized, it is the task particularly of the mother to educate her children to learn altruistic behavior and to control aggression. I would add that in the learning of control "sublimation" is most important. In this way we can turn our aggressive tendencies to good ends. Without a propensity for aggression we would not strive as we do for an achievement in accord with our hopes. For example, in writing this book we have been driven by our innate aggression to examine critically a wide range of literature, to synthesize it into meaningful stories, and to attack critically!

However, there is also a dark side to the future of human societies. As Sherrington in his last Gifford Lecture so well recognized, there is always the threat of *Homo praedatorius,* which can come in many disguises in the struggle for power that dominates so much of the society: politics, economics, and even the academic life. Always there is the insidious threat from those who avidly seek positions of power and who are concerned with their own advancement rather than the altruistic motive of making the best contribution to the culture and wellbeing of their society.

Today free societies are threatened as never before by terrorists ganging up from many countries. They may masquerade under some political guise, such as destroying the "rotten" society in which they live in order to bring about some millenarian future. Many of the "liberal left" have been blind to the dangers. But the criminal horrors of their murders, kidnapping, and plane hijacking exposes them for what they are—criminal assassins exulting in destruction and killing for its own sake, and entirely barren of any constructive ideology. At last it is being recognized that there can be no negotiation with these criminals, who are a particularly vile form of *Homo praedatorius.* They have to be fought to the death. Conor Cruise O'Brien concludes his article "Liberty and Terror": "However long it takes, the democratic struggle against the underground terrorist empires, whatever slogans they may use, is a struggle for real liberty for real people." Meanwhile there has to be some curtailment of freedom in order to preserve our society with its values.

Retrospect and Evaluation

The space traveler visiting Planet Earth again would find the marvelous transformations wrought by life that began 3,500 million years ago. Mars and the moon would still be the same arid wastes, but Planet Earth now has most of the land masses covered with vegetation—trees, grass, and shrubs. On closer inspection it would find animals on the land, in the sea, in the air. But transcending all these living creatures it would find one animal, *Homo sapiens sapiens,* who had planned and wrought great transformations so that much of the planet is controlled—the landscape with its immense areas of artificial cultivation, the controlled vegetation even of forests, and the animals now largely domesticated for use. Superimposed on this rural background are the immense constructions of cities and highways, of ships on the oceans and of airplanes and satellites above the earth. But this is but a superficial view of what is now to be exposed in depth.

The human achievements are indeed wonderful, not only in technology but more amazingly in the sciences and the humanities—the whole world of culture—and would deservedly excite admiration in our space traveler. But as it probed deeper into the human condition of the four thousand million human beings, there would be much to cause grave concern for the future. Gross inequalities in the material conditions of life in the different countries are serious enough, but of even more dire consequence would be the manner of organization and control of the human beings of those countries. In this book we are concentrating on the nature of human beings, or persons, as we shall call them, and on the necessary conditions for the fulfillment of each person as a spiritual as well as a material being. What we can call the human predicament arises from the many factors thwarting fulfillment. The economic situation is not our concern. Much literature on this already exists.

We are concerned with the deep troubles that have arisen in our society as the spiritual values on which it was built are corroded and replaced by crude materialistic motives: the quest for power by aggression and violence; the quest for pleasure with hedonism, nihilism, drug addiction, despair, suicide, all arising from the growing meaninglessness of a life bereft of its spiritual base.

Superimposed upon these societal evils is the imperialist threat of world domination or hegemony by a great empire of enslaved peoples armed with weapons of unimaginable destructiveness. For the present this threat is being uncertainly held off only by a complementary nuclear deterrence and by immense payments in food and technology—carrot-and-stick diplomacy! Thus our space traveler, while marveling at what has been accomplished on Planet Earth, would be filled with foreboding for the future, as are we the authors. So we do what we can while we can in the effort to restore faith in spiritual values so that life in a free and open society may be possible.

It may be thought that our mythical space traveler would regard the predicament of mankind on our insignificant Planet Earth as of little concern in the context of the cosmos. After all, it is no more than a medium-size planet revolving around a medium-size sun that is placed on the fringe of our great galactic system with one hundred thousand million other suns, and there are in the whole cosmos one hundred thousand million other galaxies of comparable size. We should be dwarfed to insignificance, or so it is hoped by many crude materialists, who dogmatically assert that there are countless planets harboring even more intelligent life, which may be attempting radio communication in space in the hope of discovering other intelligent life. However, space travel even to the nearest suns of our galaxy that could have planets, that could have life, that could have evolved to intelligent life, is *forever impossible*. Space scientists do listen for possible coded messages with the most sophisticated devices and are rewarded with nothing but cosmic silence! Our mythical space traveler may be deeply concerned at the human predicament. We may have here uniquely on Planet Earth a brief glimmer of self-consciousness, of spiritual values, and of creativity in an otherwise mindless and meaningless cosmos.

Suggested Readings

DOBZHANSKY, T. *The biology of ultimate concern*. New York: New American Library, 1967.

DUBOS, R. *So human an animal*. New York: Charles Scribner's Sons, 1968.

ECCLES, J. C. *Facing reality*. Heidelberg: Springer Verlag, 1970, Chs. 8,9.

ECCLES, J. C. *The human mystery*. Berlin, Heidelberg, New York: Springer Verlag Internat., 1979, Ch.6.

ECCLES, J. C. *The human psyche*. Berlin, Heidelberg, New York: Springer Verlag Internat., 1980, Chs. 8,9.

HAYEK, F. A. *The three sources of human values*. London: The London School of Economics and Political Science, 1978.

MONTAGU, A. *The nature of human aggression*. Oxford: Oxford University Press, 1976.

POPPER, K. R., and ECCLES, J. C. *The self and its brain*. Berlin, Heidelberg, New York: Springer Verlag Internat., 1977, Chs. P4, E7, Dialogue III.

SHERRINGTON, C. S. *Man on his nature*. London: Cambridge University Press, 1940.

SPERRY, R. *Science and moral priority*. New York: Columbia University Press, 1983.

THORPE, W. H. *Biology, psychology and belief*. London: Cambridge University Press, 1961.

THORPE, W. H. *Animal nature and human nature.* London: Methuen & Co., 1974.

THORPE, W. H. *Purpose in a world of chance: A biologist's view.* Oxford: Oxford University Press, 1978.

WILSON, E. O. *Sociobiology: The new synthesis.* Cambridge, Mass.: The Belknap Press, Harvard University Press, 1975.

WILSON, E. O. *On human nature.* Cambridge, Mass.: Harvard University Press, 1978.

7

Environmentalism

Since the time of Socrates utopians have recognized that there are only two kinds of manipulation available to those who would "perfect" the human race: genetic engineering and (or) the total control of one's personal and social environments. When in *Republic* Socrates is asked how the class of Guardians is to be brought into being, he replies that they will be bred like hunting dogs!

Eugenics still has its devotees, but even they will acknowledge that human beings are not likely to submit to methods of controlled and selective breeding. Moreover, since many a fool has had a genius for a son—since nearly every pedigree will turn up at least one poet and two chicken thieves—even an age as vulnerable to scientistic superstitions as ours would be hard to convert to radically hereditarian approaches to human perfectability. The male and female sex cells (gametes) each contain twenty-three pairs of chromosomes. Thus, the combinatorial possibilities that enter into the formation of an offspring are 2^{23},* a number on the order of 10,000,000. It is true

*Understand that the figure 2^{23} applies only to the simplest (and most unrepresentative) transmission of the genetic material. Once such typical processes as

enough that children have on average 50 percent of their genes in common with their parents, but it is also true that children inherit not the *traits* but the *genes* of their parents. Given the combinatorial possibilities and in light of the fact that in today's developed countries each marriage is yielding fewer than three offspring, the sheer numbers would work against the dreams of even the most sanguine eugenicist. For most utopians, then, environmentalism wins by default. And, as Socrates himself knew, even with the right hereditary "mix" only a thoroughly regimented environment could be expected to yield the sort of Guardians he had in mind.

It is important to recognize, however, that the choice of environmentalism over hereditarianism still leaves *determinism* as the ruling metaphysics. On both construals human nature is created by forces over which the individual person has no control and of which he is generally completely oblivious. On both construals *free will* is the major casualty, for its existence cannot survive the success of *either* the radical instinctivist *or* the radical environmentalist theory of human psychology.

Although every epoch of philosophical originality has hosted environmentalistic determinism, it was chiefly in the eighteenth century that the thesis became more or less "official." This was the century of both the American and the French revolutions, the century of Paine's *Rights of Man*. Especially in France, through the immensely influential writings of the *philosophes* (Voltaire, Condorcet, Helvetius, D'Alembert), the earlier empiricist psychology of John Locke was installed as a social and political truth, and one that removed all rational justifications for the existing and historical social order. Against the claims of the aristocracy the *philosophes* developed persuasive arguments to the effect that the differences among the various classes were totally determined by nothing more than traditional modes of exploitation. The Catholic Church, through its enduring connection with the monarchy, was held up to scorn and condemnation. In the social and political upheavals of the age atheism became a badge of honor. The new deity was Nature itself, and the ultimate sanctions in law, morals, politics, and commerce were to be found in what was "natural." "Through all the vocabulary of Adam," wrote Thomas Paine, "there is no such an animal as a duke or a count". Titled classes, found nowhere *in nature,* were thus dismissed as being

---

"crossing over" are included—processes allowing regions of a given chromosome to break and to unite with complementary regions of different chromosomes—the combinatorial possibilities become vastly greater than 2^{23}.

no more than "the circles drawn by the magician's wand to contract the sphere of man's felicity." In economics Adam Smith's *The Wealth of Nations* derived the theory of *laissez-faire* from the philosophy of naturalism. Jean Jacques Rousseau's "noble savage" was the celebrated *Nature-Man,* uncorrupted by the artificiality of civilization. Building on the arguments developed a century earlier by Thomas Hobbes, leading thinkers in France, Britain, and America insisted that all the forms and policies of government be justified on naturalistic grounds. Since the common quest of all men is *naturally* for survival, for possessions, and for happiness, it follows that the only rationale for government arises from just these pursuits. Rousseau and (earlier) Locke had advanced theories of the *social contract* to account for the historical tendency of human aggregates to surrender their rights and powers to the monarch or ruling party, a *quid pro quo* contract that imposed at least implicit duties on the sovereign. David Hume—closer in his political theory to Mao—rejected the contract theory but reinforced the general proposition according to which government, in all its variety, originates in totally natural contexts and retains its power through the sentiments of the governed, especially the sentiment of fear!

The philosophy of one age often becomes the ideology of the next. In the nineteenth century the program of the *philosophes* was transformed from theory to practice. The naturalism of the eighteenth century was divided, flourishing as *Romanticism* in aesthetic quarters and *Materialism* in scientific or quasiscientific quarters. Radical forms of each prospered in Germany, where Romanticism was nurtured by Goethe, Schiller, and Hölderlin and Materialism would become the watchword of the left-wing neo-Hegelians, Feuerbach and Marx. In Britain, less inclined than Germany toward "metaphysics," the Reform Acts of the 1830s and the political writings of John Stuart Mill both gave expression to the naturalistic and environmentalistic determinism of the *philosophes.* And in America, in the "Age of Jackson," the Plain Man was installed as a veritable arbiter of truth!

It is of less importance that Mill's influential works defended liberalism and individualism and that Marx's heralded socialsim and communalism. Both Mill and Marx subscribed to a *psychological determinism* according to which all social and political institutions were to be understood as arising from purely historical and "material" conditions of life—the life of actual persons in real situations. Marx, unlike Mill, was an innocent in the area of philosophy of mind. (His doctoral dissertation on Epicurus educated him in the psychological materialism of Pierre Gassendi, the seventeenth-century popularizer of Epicureanism and Descartes's most accomplished critic). Marx thus devoted little attention to the analysis of individual psychology, judging the matter to have been settled in favor of matter! Mill, on the other hand, was not a polemicist but a philosopher and required of his own political philosophy that it stand on a valid model of human psychology. He thought he had found this model in *associationism,* the doctrine whereby all of mental life arises out of assemblies of prior and current experiences, "associated together" by the laws of repetition, practice, reward, and punishment. He was thus able to locate the sources of mental life in the external environment, countering the claims of the *a priori* school. According to the *a priori* school, any number of fundamental "truths" were accessible only to an "intuitive faculty" and were neither based on nor to be challenged by the mere data of experience. Put simply, Mill's position was that the content of consciousness—the entire fabric of mental life—arises from experience such that every truth claim can be settled only by observation, measurement, and the principles of inductive logic. The affairs of the world, including the moral and political, are not discoverable by deduction, cannot be "intuited," and are not possessed by a privileged few.

Mill was well aware of the traps determinists set for themselves and was candid enough not to trivialize them. He made distinctions between his own deterministic psychology and what he called "Asiatic Fatalism," though he never did relax the tension between his own system and this very fatalism. Mill was, after all, a practical philosopher eager to reform the thinking of his age. Yet read in a certain light, his environmentalistic psychology would seem to predispose his readers to accept or reject his philosophy according to their own history of associations. If, indeed, the mind is completely furnished by experience, and if our thoughts are but reflections of our own personal histories, then our reaction to any set of proposals, including Mill's, is determined.

In attempting to avoid the paradox of a deterministic reformism, Mill found it necessary to postulate something he referred to as *human character,* which (somehow) provided the basis upon which we might take matters into our own hands and improve our lot. But if this ability is, alas, a reflection of our (mental-cognitive) *freedom,* then our associational histories do not determine the contents and modes of thought, and, accordingly, Mill's psychology is defective. Yet it was just this psychology that was designed to refute the *a priori* school of politics and morals. Mill's dilemma, which is the dilemma faced by all determinists, is that his exhortations are pointless unless his theory of psychology is wrong!

If Mill's psychology was defective, Marx's was fatally simplistic, assuming as it did that human "consciousness" is fabricated out of the pattern of economic forces and "modes of production" that have operated throughout the history of civilization. It is not necessary here to recount the number of failed predictions emanating from Marxist economic theory, nor is it worth exploring the enormity of the miseries spawned by the several large-scale attempts to govern according to orthodox Marxist (or Marxist-Leninist) principles. It is sufficient here merely to acknowledge that single-cause theories of the human person are doomed to the category of the ridiculous, no matter how solemnly they are advanced or rapturously adopted.

Following Feuerbach, Marx was satisfied that "God" was a human invention possessed of attributes and powers by which religion could come to serve as "the opiate of the masses." The historical function of religion, on this account, is to keep the downtrodden at peace with the exploiting class by promising the former the long-term rewards of the hereafter. In Western civilization especially the great age of Christianity was regarded by Marx as suppressive, apologetical, insidious, and self-serving. By keeping the attention of the proletariat fixed on transcendent considerations, religion was able to serve the most important mission of the privileged class, which was, alas, the preservation of privilege. Communism, however, would devote its energies to the human *here and now* and would, through the machinery of class revolts, equip citizens to discover and protect their real earthly interests.

By way of a systematic misunderstanding of Hegel's concept of *alienation,* Marxist theorists attempted to explain the problems of the world in terms of the distance industrialization had placed between human labor and the fruits of that labor. Modern modes of production had created special classes, cut off from each other, but ultimately united in the sense of forming that homogeneous *proletariat* manipulated in such a way as to produce wealth for the *bourgeois* and their aristocratic patrons. But the latter too formed an exploited class by virtue of having its entire identity tied up in purely commercial modes of expression. We learn in the *Communist Manifesto* that all this will be swept away and replaced by "an association in which the free development of each is the condition for the free development of all."

The tide that will be reversed is that which ushered in "the distribution of labor" that confined each person to a narrow sphere of productivity from which he could escape only at the cost of his livelihood. Now so confined, the person can have no identity but that established by his labor speciality. Moreover, since he is paid less than the worth of his labor—as this worth is revealed in the actual selling of the products of his labor—it is essential to the formation of capital by the wealthy classes that he be kept in his place. Political and legal devices are therefore constructed to maintain the division of labor and guarantee its surpluses. Governed by economic motivations, the power elite cannot be expected to change their ways voluntarily, so only revolutionary upheavals will lead to the communistic utopia.

Marx's own predictions of the date on which capitalism would fall were all overtaken by history. It didn't fall in 1848 (his earliest prediction) or in 1870, and it is still very much alive in 1984. Furthermore, it does not seem to become weaker as a result of the proletariat's learning ever more about the world and themselves. Capitalism has not survived because its "victims" have been kept in a state of ignorance or innocence. Nor has socialism—the intermediate stage on the way to true communism—given any signs of retreating in the face of "historical inevitabilities." It would seem that Marxism attracts the sort of disciple who shares Marx's own one-sided and contemptuous view of human persons; the sort of disciple who, once in power, justifies unbending authoritarianism by tying it to a theory of psychology that regards men and women as unfit to determine their own destinies.

If Poland's Solidarity movement does not satisfy the Marxist concept of a revolt by the working class, nothing does. The brutal suppression of that movement, many have said, shows that the Soviet dictators are not "true Marxists." But it shows something far more revealing; it shows that they *cannot* be Marxists without inviting the utter demise of Marxism. For if they were willing to permit the "proletariat" throughout the Soviet bloc to choose lives and governments for themselves—to combine their powers and force the state to yield—the earliest casualty in most countries would be Marxism itself. It is not merely coincidental that in *every* country in which Marxist theory is the official theory of government the durability of the system is preserved by a rigorous system of police security guaranteed by force of arms. The standards Marx himself insisted on applying were those of "realism." Equipped with such standards, the disinterested observer would have to conclude that Marxism is a flawed and failed

conception of human nature, a conception anchored to a pitifully je-
june understanding of just what gives us all our sense of dignity,
worth, and preciousness. What it is, of course, are those attributes
that *rise above* the merely natural order and that cannot be explained in
the impoverished language of materialism and environmentalism.
To the extent that religion is an "opiate," it has not been restricted to
the "masses." Kings and despots, millionaires and tribal chieftains,
philosophers and fools have found it irresistible. That some have used
our longing for transcendence for purposes of exploitation merely re-
inforces the claim that this longing arises from our deepest and most
natural sentiments. These sentiments, properly understood, may
constitute the only grounds on which all of us may be said to be
"equal." They surely do constitute some of the grounds on which we
may be said to be *free*—free to pursue that which has no empirically
verifiable existence and which enters into no material-causal sequence. It is in our very morality—even our "bourgeois morality"—
that we recognize the ultimate authority of *principle* and thus recognize ourselves as *having to choose*. This is the evidence of our freedom,
and, from the perspective of any adequate theory of human nature, it
makes no difference whether we are in fact free or only "think" we
are. Matter doesn't think it is, for matter doesn't think.

Moral choice proceeds from what is commonly called *conscience*.
It was Marx's burden within a sociological context and Sigmund
Freud's within the psychoanalytic context of individual psychology to
show that this conscience is instilled—from the outside—by the process of *socialization*. Unlike Marx, Freud entered professional life with
Darwin's theory of evolution firmly established within scientific circles. For Freud, therefore, the power of the environment to create entirely new species was sufficient proof that we too are created *in toto* by
purely natural processes. Like Marx, Freud argued that the person's
identity—his *ego*—was formed by external conditions beyond his control and comprehension. By virtue of our animalistic ancestry we are
"naturally" self-preserving, self-gratifying creatures who must be
"socialized." Here again, however, the consequence is *alienation,* this
time between the manufactured social self and the instinctual real
self. The former arises out of the repression of the latter, and thus
neurosis is the price paid for civilization. The unresolved *Oedipal complex,* which identifies one's mother as the ideal object of sexual gratification and, in the process, puts sons at unconscious war with their
fathers, gives rise to religion and its rituals: the ritual sacrificing of the
father-figure, ritual totem-worship, belief in the "rebirth" that fol-

lows the death of God, and the deep and lifelong sense of guilt rooted in the unconscious impulse to parricide.

It has been said, and not without justification, that psychoanalysis invented a theory of human nature and then invented facts that would support the theory. Freud's "universal" totemism was known at the time not to be a universal feature of religions either primitive or developed. This is but an illustrative point, for it would take many, many pages to list the Freudian claims that are either disconfirmed by established facts or utterly unconfirmable by any fact. There are interesting parallels between psychoanalytic theory and the deep psychological distress candidly revealed in Freud's autobiographical writings, but this suggests no more than that Freud himself had certain problems of a "Freudian" nature. We can have sympathy for his suffering without including ourselves as victims of the same "instinctual" impulses.

Rousseau had bequeathed a noble savage, but psychoanalytic theory bequeaths only the savage. What the Rousseauan and Freudian bequests have in common is the (alleged) price exacted by civilization, the price of *alienation,* the loss of the freedom *to be ourselves.* In the Enlightenment this freedom was thought to be the gift of rational government organized around the established and the evolving facts and methods of natural science. A deeper and darker source of freedom was seen by Rousseau, and in this respect he is more the nineteenth-century Romantic than the eighteenth-century Rationalist. With Marxist materialism the epoch of naturalistic rationalism reached its culmination, only to be displaced by the Freudian and Darwinian naturalistic *irrationalsim*—naturalism gone Gothic. Marx had intended to dedicate one of his works to Darwin, convinced that "dialectical materialism" had found confirmation in Darwin's great scientific achievement.* Freud too singled out Darwin as especially influential in his own development as a theorist. What Marx found in Darwinian theory were just those earthy and utterly material conditions of life that shape the character of every species, whereas Freud found the arguments he needed to "verify" the animalistic and instinctual equipment of the unconscious. Exploited by the class system, Marxist Man lives the inauthentic life of a slave, drugged into submission by the myths of religion. Exploited by the processes of "socialization," Freudian Man lives the inauthentic life of a neurotic, self-drugged by a conscience skillfully crafted to conceal the real

---

*Darwin's declination was characteristically polite.

urges and passions of the self behind the mask. The liberation of Marxist Man comes about only after a genuine class-consciousness is developed so that he can see the historical-material forces that have relegated him to the status of a pawn. The liberation of Freudian Man follows only the prolonged and guided *psycho*analysis that exposes to consciousness those repressed energies bequeathed by evolution, which is to say by historical-material forces.

On both of these constricted and finally question-begging accounts, the concepts of freedom and liberation are undefined or, when defined, wrongly defined. The contemporary American behaviorist B. F. Skinner avoids the dilemma by arguing that we move *Beyond Freedom and Dignity* and simply accept the fact that "human nature," if the term means anything at all, is no more than that constellation of perceptions and behaviors brought about by personal histories of rewards and punishments or "reinforcements." But the dilemma cannot be averted so easily, for Skinner too has *exhorted* us to *adopt* a particular theory and has thereby accepted that we are *free* to do so. What his writings have in common with Marxist and Freudian interpretations of life is the conviction that we have been determined *from the outside* by the process of socialization, a process that has been ineffective, often exploitative, and largely unbeknownst to the creatures thus "shaped." What is common, therefore, is the *historical-materialist determinism* that denies or depreciates human initiative, individuality, inspiration, genius, and transcendence—in a word, *free will.*

The conflict between free will and determinism is fully examined as early as Plato's *Republic,* where man is spoken of as a puppet, moved and jostled by the gods. There is, however, one string that each person can pull back on, successfully resisting even Olympian forces, and that is "the golden string of reason."

The ancient philosophers found deep metaphysical significance in this issue, but to later Christian teachers it was of even greater importance. On the Christian interpretation of life, each person is endowed with a unique soul whose eternal fate is decided by the way that person lives his earthly life. There is, then, complete *personal responsibility* for one's actions. Yet, on this same interpretation of life, man is blessed by the concerns of a providential God who is at once omniscient and omnipotent. The problem, at least as it has been framed by Christian theologians for the past millennuim, is to reconcile God's unlimited knowledge, power, and goodness to the fact of man's moral freedom. If God is omniscient, there must be full knowledge of everything we *shall* ever do. If God is omnipotent, there must be the potential for causing us to act or not to act. And if there is, at the same time, limitless benevolence, then the power of God would have to be exerted in the interest of causing only good and preventing all evil. Nonetheless, man does act in evil ways. Thus (the argument goes), God is limited in power or in prescience or in benevolence. And to be *limited* is, alas, to be less than God.

We shall not, of course, undertake to "solve" the most vexing and tangled mysteries of Christian theology. We enter the controversy only to remind the reader of the centrality of the *free will–determinism* issue to religious thought and to account for the scholarly efforts that have been expended on it by theologians. As early as the thirteenth century, chiefly through the genius of Thomas Aquinas, the issue was "settled" to a degree that removed at least some of the apparent paradox. We mention some of the highlights of this partial solution by way of introducing contemporary versions of the issue.

Let us begin with the proposition that man's wrongdoing establishes that God is lacking in power or in foresight or in goodness. First, there is all the difference between withholding one's power and not having the power. That God *does not* completely determine our actions does not prove that He cannot. Second, from the fact that what we will do is known to another, it does not follow that our actions are in any way *determined*. We may know, for example, that a certain flight has been canceled by the airline, and this information may come to us while Smith is driving to the airport. We *know* he will return home after discovering there is no alternative flight so that travel this day is impossible, but the actions he comes to take are not *determined* by our foreknowledge. Thus, to establish that God is omnipotent and omniscient is not, in itself, enough to establish that human actions are divinely determined.

This leaves us with that great theological conundrum, *the problem of evil,* which is voiced in many keys. We shall set aside the death of babies or the suffering of the sick and all related "natural" events. These, properly understood, are regrettable but are not *evils* unless we argue further that a specific agent has set out to *cause* them. If, instead, they are the inevitable consequence of the natural, material world as it is given, then death and suffering are no more "evil" than the tides, the weather, the mountains, and the trees. The difficult version of the problem comes from deliberate acts of human wickedness. How, it is asked, can an all-powerful and all-benevolent God *permit* man to commit palpably unjust acts against innocent persons? And the answer, which is so obvious as to seem erroneous, is that it is impossible—it is *logically impossible*—to attach responsibility for actions over which the actor has absolutely no control. To the extent that we are morally responsible for what we do, we *must* be free to do it. Even God cannot violate the law of contradiction!

Entire libraries can be filled with treatises on this matter, so we say no more. When Thomas Aquinas set his keen intelligence on the question, he was able to unearth several proofs of the freedom of man's will, and one of these will have a very modern ring: *the effects of exhortations and rewards and punishments.* Note that today's radical environmentalist—the radical behavioristic psychologist—concludes from the efficacy of rewards and punishments that we are determined by our environment in all our actions; taking the same facts, Thomas Aquinas arrives at just the opposite conclusion. Who is right?

The Thomistic conclusion is grounded in common sense. The only way strong exhortations or rewards or punishments might possibly influence the course of human activity is if persons are inclined to *choose* rewards and *intentionally* to avoid punishments. To be moved by rhetoric and other hortatory inducements is to be able "to change one's mind," to be *persuaded* or *converted* or *reasoned with* or *convinced.* But words such as these virtually entail a free agent. The rock rolling down a mountainside cannot be diverted by rhetoric or induced by sweets. It cannot be talked out of its journey or rationally appealed to or persuaded to a different path. The point is that the efficacy of "reinforcement" in affecting human behavior, far from proving that the will is not free, is but another piece of evidence in favor of this very freedom.

In response to this the radical environmentalist may agree that we are, at least in a manner of speaking, "free" to choose pleasure over pain but may argue that our choices here are so thoroughly built into our very nature that, for all practical purposes, our conduct is nothing but the consequence of prior, current, and possible pleasures. We are completely "shaped" by our environments in that, as pleasure-seeking and pain-avoiding creatures, we can be rendered entirely predictable once our "reinforcement histories" are known or controlled. The most relevant difference between, for example, a Justice of the Supreme Court and an ordinary vagrant are the environmental differences in their respective backgrounds. Heredity counts for something, but by and large the immense differences among otherwise physiologically normal persons are to be understood as arising from differences in training (conditioning). Were the jurist and the vagrant to swap biographies, they would thereby swap current identities.

Two very popular implications emerge from this thesis. There is first the moral relativism we have already discussed and, we hope, disposed of. What was to make all morals *relative* are just those differing histories of reinforcement that give rise to different "values." By the radical environmentalist's lights, we could just as easily "shape" children to be homicidal maniacs as we now generally "shape" them to be law-abiding citizens. Accordingly, both the criminal and the man of virtue are but expressions of environmentally induced inclinations. The second implication is, of course, that no one actually *deserves* either the praises or the blames, the advantages or the disadvantages now so unevenly dispersed in the world. Since every psychologically (read *behaviorally*) unique thing about us has been "programmed" into us by a history of rewards and punishments, we are worthy of neither celebrity nor denunciation for our actions. In a word, we are not *responsible*.

Like materialism and its associated robot theory, there is something of the liar's paradox in all this. It should, after all, be quite useless to prevail upon our intelligences in order to secure our approval of a theory of this sort if the theory, in fact, requires that our entire psychological makeup—including our *willingness* to *weigh* propositions of this kind—is already determined. Indeed, how can we distinguish between a scientific theory and the strange "reinforcement history" that gets our protagonist to defend radical environmentalism? If the theory is correct, we will never really know, because by its very terms any ultimate *assent* we give to it must also be the result of "shaping." What do we say to a person who insists that all of our choices, beliefs, mental acts, perceptions, motives, and the like have been "programmed" into us? When we notify him that we often harbor very unpopular views or that we have suffered for some of our convictions or that we routinely deny ourselves all sorts of pleasures on the grounds that they are unworthy objects of our commitment, he quickly replies that these too—our views, our convictions, our self-denials—have been "programmed." And to prove his point he will unfurl the findings from studies of animal conditioning and (even) the conditioning of certain human actions.

The fact is, there is really nothing we can say, not because the radical environmentalist has made his case, but because he hasn't really said anything admitting of scientific testing. He might just as well contend that the universe, including all existing human beings with their memories and knowledge, came into being twenty years ago. If we point to the Egyptian pyramids, he will tell us that they, too, were brought into being only twenty years ago but were made to seem thousands of years old. What makes his account similar to this preposterous one is that our personal memories are not good enough to provide us with direct proofs to the contrary. The radical environmentalist has most of the "shaping" going on during a person's earliest days and months of life. Thus when the *adult* claims that his parents didn't reward action X or punish action Y, the radical environmentalist is likely to insist that all this occurred during "formative" times of which the reporter is now oblivious. And, on another version of the theory, we are also unable to refute the thesis because what it amounts to is a denial of our own authority to account for what in fact are our motives. The hero who risks his life so that others might live is said to be working for "approval," a kind of "social reinforcement" effectively employed by parents to "shape" children into sociable beings. If our hero (uncharacteristically) insists that he was moved by nothing less than a love of his fellow man, by the desire to do the *right* thing, he can always be rebutted on the grounds that that is why he *thinks* he acted bravely. His "reinforcement history" also included such justificatory rationalizations. But the reason he *desired* to do what he did is that actions of this sort were routinely reinforced during his childhood and were socially applauded since that time.

Thus does the FOO (fallacy of origins) return one more time, here confusing the method by which conscience is initially forged with the later actions that will proceed from a fully developed and personally managed conscience. It is entirely possible that Billy is "shaped" not to pull the dog's tail by parents who greet such actions with disapproval. In this case we account for Billy's altered behavior in terms of his desire to avoid parental disapproval. But thirty years later, when we find the fully grown Billy arguing against cruelty toward animals, are we still entitled to use the same account? We learn from this adult not that he is eager to avoid parental disapproval but that there are principled reasons for caring for defenseless creatures. He may go so far as to recall his own childhood conduct and to recognize what stood behind his parents' remonstrances. But it would be fatuous to propose that the adult's ethical position is somehow "like" the child's obedience to a parental command. To know that a building, in a manner of speaking, "began" as a collection of bricks is to know very little about it as a building, and nothing about what distinguishes it from other brick buildings. Again, it is like being told that we all began as zygotes. It is an uninformative fact laboring to become a sublime truth, and its failure is rooted in the fallacy of its major premise: that the origin of an entity or state or condition contains everything that will later be true of it. This is the *fallacy of origins,* which, far from being a "progressive" doctrine, would sanction the most heinous forms of the *status quo.* To strip persons of responsibility is finally to strip collectives of persons of theirs. It is to abandon every reason, every justification for improving the lot of the disadvantaged. At the end of its quasi-ethical tether, it makes this "the best of all possible worlds" by making this the only possible world; the world "shaped" by its own history of rewards and punishments. But the world's history tells against this thesis and shows often and dramatically the extraordinary power we have over the environment and, through it, over ourselves. Everything we know about ourselves tends to refute radical versions of environmentalism. It is one of the colossal superstitions of our age and has long since lost the right to command our allegiance.

Suggested Readings

DAVIS, L. H. *Theory of action.* Englewood Cliffs, N. J.: Prentice-Hall, 1979.

ROBINSON, D. N. *An intellectural history of psychology* (Rev. ed.). New York: Macmillan, 1981.

ROBINSON, D. N. *Toward a science of human nature: Essays on the psychologies of Hegel, Mill, Wundt and James.* New York: Columbia University Press, 1982.

RYLE, G. *The concept of mind.* London: Hutchinson, 1949.

SKINNER, B. F. *Science and human behavior.* New York: Macmillan, 1956.

WATSON, J. B. *Psychology from the standpoint of a behaviorist.* Philadelphia: Lippincott, 1919.

8

Language, Thought, and Brain

The Levels of Language

We recognize the qualities of personhood in one another by reciprocal communication in one or another linguistic mode. Such communication is the very essence of society. At the highest levels human languages are most important constituents of World 3 and play a key role in the development of each human person in the interaction World 2 ⇌ World 3 on the "ladder of personhood" (Figure 3-4).

The most comprehensive scope of all that can be subsumed in the category of language is that formulated by Karl Bühler in 1930 and further developed by Karl Popper. It is important that animal languages are considered along with human languages. Usually in a language there is a sender, a means of communication, and a receiver. It is a special kind of semiotic system.

In the Bühler–Popper classification (Figure 8-1) there are two lower forms of language (1 and 2) that animal and human languages

FUNCTIONS	VALUES	
(4) Argumentative Function	validity/ invalidity	
(3) Descriptive Function	falsity truth	
(2) Signal Function	efficiency/ inefficiency	} MAN
(1) Expressive Function	revealing/ not revealing	

FIGURE 8-1. The Four Levels of the Bühler-Popper Classification of Language. Functions and associated values are shown. It will be maintained that we share with animals only the two lower functions.

have in common and two higher forms (3 and 4) that may be uniquely human, though this is contested, as we shall see later. Meanwhile it can be agreed that the two lower forms of languages are:

1. *The expressive or symptomatic function:* The animal is expressing its inner states of emotion or feeling, as also is done by human beings with calls, cries, laughter, and so forth.

2. *The releasing or signaling function of language:* The "sender" by some communication attempts to bring about some reaction in the "receiver." For example, the alarm call of a bird signals danger to the flock. Ethological studies have revealed an enormous variety of these signals, particularly in the social animals. In communication between humans and animals, there is a large variety of signaling, as for example with pets or between a man and his sheepdog or a person and a horse. But the unspoken communications between persons are enormously greater. Think of all the signaling by gestures with eyes, hands, face, and lips at all levels of subtlety and intimacy. A person can communicate so much without talking. Think for example of the signaling of anger and contempt.

The two higher levels are:

3. *The descriptive function of language* makes up the greater part of human communication. We describe to others our experiences, for example, the effect of weather on the garden; the prices and quality of articles in the shops; our recent travel; the behavior of children, friends, or neighbors; recent happenings in politics, achievements in technology, or discoveries in science—the list is endless. It is important to recognize that the two lower functions of language are

associated with utterances that are both expressions and signals. The unique feature of the descriptive function of the language is that the statements may be factually true or factually false. The possibility of lying is implicit.

4. *The argumentative function* was not in the original Bühler triad and was added by Popper. It is language at its highest level. With its sophisticated character it was certainly the last to develop phylo-genetically, and this is mirrored ontogenetically. The art of critical argument is intimately bound up with the human ability to think rationally.

The four levels of language are well illustrated in the development from baby to child, where there is progressive conquest of levels from the initial purely expressive level to the signaling level, then to the descriptive level and eventually to the argumentative level. It is important to recognize that each level of language is permeated by the lower levels. For example, when arguing there is expression of feelings, signaling by gestures in the attempt to convert the antagonist, and description in underpinning the arguments by factual reference.

The above accounts have been permeated by the dualist-interactionist philosophy. In contrast, as Popper states:

> The physicalist will try to give a physical explanation—a causal explanation—of language phenomena. This is equivalent to interpreting language as expressive of the state of the speaker, and therefore as having the expressive function alone. . . . But the consequences of this are disastrous. For if all language is seen as merely expression and communication, then one neglects all that is characteristic of human language in contradistinction to animal language: its ability to make true and false statements, and to produce valid and invalid arguments. This, in its turn, has the consequence that the physicalist is prevented from accounting for the difference between propaganda, verbal intimidation, and rational argument.

Similarly the behaviorist fails because he recognizes nothing above the signal function of language (level 2).

Linguistic Expression

In its subjective sense the word "thought" refers to a mental experience or a mental process. We may call it a "thought process," and it has a World 2 status (Figure 3-1). In contrast there is the world of the products of thought processes, the world of human creativity, which is World 3 (Figure 3–3). In linguistic expression subjective thought processes achieve an objective status (World 3) and on very special occasions the linguistic expression may attain to a high aesthetic status, as for example in an ode by John Keats.

Descartes emphasized the relationship between language and thought and also the creativity of thoughts in linguistic expression, which is uniquely human. He attributed this human uniqueness to the operation of a new principle, the human soul, upon the brain, which was associated with the power to reason and was lacking in the animals. This corresponds to the new principle proposed by Chomsky in the creativity of linguistic usage.

Before considering further this creative operation by which subjective thought processes become expressed in language that may even be an artistic creation, it is necessary to give the outlines of the operations by which well-formed sentences are created. As Chomsky has claimed, the construction of a sentence is a unique happening. In the course of a conversation we can all form unique sentences never before created. In fact, we have the capacity to create an infinite variety of sentences.

Verbal expression in language can be considered at three levels. First is the need for an adequate, well-understood vocabulary of all the various parts of speech, the lexicon. Second is the process of correctly arranging the words according to grammatical rules, which is the syntactic requirement. The criterion is that sentences are judged to be well formed by experienced natural speakers of the language. Third, the sentences have to be judged as meaningful, which is the criterion of semantics. Sentences with a satisfactory syntactical structure may nevertheless be nonsensical. I give an example from Chomsky: "Colourless green ideas sleep furiously."

These criteria of a human language will be crucial in assessing later how far the trained apes have been able to exhibit traces of what can be recognized as a human language, that is, language at level 3 or at level 4.

The Learning of a Human Language

As noted in Chapter 2, even in the first months of life a baby is continually practicing its vocal organs and is beginning thus to learn this most complex of all motor coordinations. Vocal learning is guided by hearing and is at first imitative of sounds heard; this leads on to the simplest words, of the type "dada," "papa," "mama," which are produced at about one year. It is important to recognize that speech is dependent on the feedback from hearing spoken words. The deaf are mute. In linguistic development recognition outstrips expression. A child has a veritable word hunger, asking for names and practicing incessantly even when alone. It dares to make mistakes devolving from its own rules, as for example with the irregular plurals of nouns. Language does not come about by simple imitation. The child abstracts regularities and relations from what it hears and applies these syntactic principles in building up its linguistic expressions. The earliest stages of functional development may be almost entirely *pragmatic*, as the child uses his protolanguage to regulate those around him, to acquire desirables, and to invite interaction. Those protofunctions develop into the more mature *mathetic* function, in which the child uses language to learn about the world—its cognitive aspect. But of course these two functions, the pragmatic and the mathetic, are inextricably mixed in the language that a child uses from moment to moment.

Amazing self-organizing processes are employed by children. We would suggest that the remarkable linguistic progress by the child in the first few years is attributable to the developing self-consciousness of the child in its struggle for self-realization and self-expression. Its mental development and its linguistic development are in reciprocal positive interaction. A necessary condition of human language may prove to be the ability to symbolize *oneself.*

When normally hearing children have two congenitally deaf parents, they hear no language from them, and their own vocalizations have no effect in obtaining what they want. Yet these children begin to speak at the usual time and show normal speech development. Presumably this occurs because the chance encounters outside the home are sufficient guides to learning. Thus by its linguistic capacity the child avails itself of what is provided by the environment, limited though it may be. To be able to speak given even minimal exposure to speech is part of our biological heritage. This endowment of propensities and sensitivities has a genetic foundation (cf. Figure 6–1), but one cannot speak of genes of language. On the other hand, far beyond our present understanding, we can assume that the genes do provide coded instructions for the building of the special areas of the cerebral cortex concerned with language as well as all the subsidiary structures concerned in verbalization. These structural features will be considered later.

The general diagram of evolution (Figure 6-1) shows a sharp separation between Biological Evolution to the left, entirely within World 1, and Cultural Evolution to the right, entirely within World 3. It shows that the human brain is built by the genetic code with the *propensity* for language and that any human language can be learned. The language heard is the language learned. Chapter 6 made reference to the application of Figure 6-1 to the whole range of human propensities for culture. Brains in World 1, using conscious learning, a World 2 performance, store the culture in World 3, as has been diagrammed in Figure 3-4.

The Language Training of Apes

Descartes proposed that there was a qualitative difference between man and animals, as displayed partly by language. Animals were automata lacking anything equivalent to human self-consciousness. They communicated by a limited vocabulary of signs but lacked speech in which language conveyed and molded thoughts. Human beings were guided by reason, animals by instinct, and to Descartes human language was an activity of the human soul. The Darwinian revolution established the phylogenetic status of man as a primate and a near relative of the apes. It became an attractive research program to show that in *every respect* there was a continuity, with merely quantitative differences. The one obstacle in this smooth transition was the uniqueness of human language. There was apparently a clear *qualitative* difference between human language and the ape languages, which qualified only at the two lower levels of Figure 8-1. Hence a whole series of research programs designed to demonstrate the linguistic abilities of apes and to establish that the difference is merely quantitative have come into being. Their success would mean elimination of the gap in the phylogeny and the establishment of an "evolutionary continuity." Robert Brown vividly expresses the motivation: "Why does anyone care? For the same reason, perhaps, that we care about space travel. It is lonely being the only language-using species in the universe. We want a chimp to talk so that we can say: 'Hello, out there. What's it like, being a chimpanzee?'"

The initial projects were a series of valiant attempts by Furness, the Hayeses and Kellogg to teach apes to articulate when brought up in a human family. Even after years the achievement was only four words: papa, mama, cup, up! Lieberman attributed this failure to the anatomical defects of the ape's vocal apparatus, which limited the articulation of some vowels. However, human beings with gross lesions of the vocal apparatus—for example, the entire loss of larynx or of tongue—are still able to speak despite these great disabilities. Also various experimental disturbances of the human vocal apparatus can be compensated by remarkable adjustments. A normal human vocal tract in itself is neither necessary nor sufficient to account for the unique linguistic ability of humans, which was Descartes's conclusion.

The failure to train apes in vocal language has led to a variety of projects utilizing other training procedures. These projects have generated an enormous interest, because it seemed there would be a breakthrough of the barrier between man and other animals. At the same time there have been systematic studies of apes in their natural habitat, as for example Jane Goodall with the chimpanzees in the Gombe Stream Reserve. In 1980 Thomas Sebeok and Jean Umiker-Sebeok of the University of Indiana published a remarkable documentation of these ape language projects as provided by the investigators and also the critical evaluation of the reports of these projects by a number of linguistic experts. Furthermore the experimentalists just as strongly have criticized each other! I have the distinct impression that this criticism has provided a much-needed catharsis in a field that has suffered from too much publicity.

The most extensive and elaborate attempt to demonstrate linguistic ability in apes is that carried out since 1966 by the Gardners using American Sign Language (ASL) so as to give the chimpanzees the advantage of using a hand signal system that relates to their natural gestural communication. Thus apes have the opportunity to display their ability to learn a language without handicap by their alleged vocal inadequacy. The young female chimpanzee, Washoe, has been the subject of most of their investigations over many years. More recently there have been three additions. In all her waking hours Washoe was in human company that communicated by ASL among themselves as well as to Washoe. She achieved a vocabulary of 130 signs and could arrange them in strings of up to four "words." Almost all of the signed messages were requests for food or social attention, so it is an instrumental communication pragmatically oriented. By contrast, child language is largely concerned with enquiring and learning about the "world," the mathetic function referred to above.

In the first year and a half the chimp babies may be ahead of human babies in learning a sign language, but by two years the child vocabulary is larger. However, the mere size of the vocabulary is not an acceptable criterion of linguistic ability, which must be judged on the way in which the words are used. There is no doubt that the chimps can convey intended meanings, that is, they exhibit in their ASL a semantic ability. However, there is doubt whether any syntactic rules are obeyed by the strings of signs (words) produced by the chimps. For example, signs for "me," "tickle," and "you" are arranged in every possible order to give the same request, namely, "you tickle me." By contrast a child of three already has ideas of syntax in forming sentences appropriate for making demands, commands, negations, and questions.

There have been criticisms of this pioneering work of the Gardners. For example, there is a danger of overinterpretation of the signing by the ape, even though the Gardners have set up very stringent criteria. A more serious criticism is that the signing by the apes may be dependent on unconscious signals from the trainer, that is, the performance is often a Clever-Hans effect (named after the horse whose additions and subtractions were found to depend on unwitting cues given by the trainer). It was optimistically hoped that a competent "signer" such as Washoe would be keen to teach the sign language to naive chimps showing only a rudimentary performance. However, there was only a minimal intraspecific communication by signing. Furthermore, the hope that Washoe would teach ASL to her offspring was disappointed. This failure of intraspecific teaching makes one question whether in fact these ASL-trained apes greatly value it as a means of communication.

What then have these investigations with ASL demonstrated? There is first the ability of the apes to learn signs for things and actions. Second, they can use this symbolism in an instrumental way to signal requests for food and pleasurable experience, and to give expression to their feelings. Thus this communication by ASL falls into the two lower categories of language (Figure 8-1). There is no clear evidence that it is used in a descriptive manner even at such a simple level as "dog bites cat" and its transformation, "cat is bitten by dog."

In order to test more clearly and systematically the abilities of apes to learn a symbolic communication having some relation to language, David Premack developed a most ingenious system using plastic chips as symbols for words. The colors and shapes of these chips give the reference, that is a particular word or thing is specified by a chip of a particular shape and color. The method of training is operant conditioning, with rewards for success. In this way a young female chimp, Sarah, has been able to develop a vocabulary for objects, colors, action words ("insert," "take"), and the preposition "on." Premack has very cleverly utilized these procedures to study the ability of the ape to learn and discriminate. However, there has been much criticism of these experiments. The tests reported by Eric Lenneberg are of particular relevance. He trained normal high school students with the procedures described by Premack, replicating Premack's study as literally as possible. Two human subjects were quickly able to achieve considerably lower error scores than those reported for the chimpanzee but were unable to translate correctly into English a single sentence they had formed. In fact, they did not understand that there was any correspondence between the plastic symbols and language. They were under the impression that their task was to solve puzzles!

In an attempt to utilize computer techniques to teach symbolic communication to chimpanzees, Duane Rumbaugh has developed a most sophisticated teaching machine that was essentially two twenty-five-key consoles, each key symbolizing a word or phrase. In essentials the procedure resembles that of Premack with its use of symbols but is designed so as to store all the key operations by the chimp (Lana) around the clock. The arrangement was specially designed for requesting food, drink, and services, but this had to be done in the correct grammatical form of the language designed for the system. As with Premack's investigations on Sarah, we think Lana's communications are all in the two lowest levels of language (cf. Figure 8–1).

In the summary of all these experimental attempts to teach language to apes, it can be said that a remarkable ability to learn symbolic communication has been demonstrated. This communication is used by the apes pragmatically—to request food or social contacts. It is not used mathetically for the purpose of learning about the surrounding world, as is done very effectively by a three-year-old child. There is no doubt that apes are adept at learning symbolic languages at level 2, that is, as signals, but it is doubtful that they ever manage to rise to level 3, descriptive language, and of course level 4 is out of the question. These characteristic features of human language have not been displayed by apes, even after the most painstaking teaching procedures. Apes can use language semantically, particularly in ASL, but there is no clear evidence that their linguistic expressions have syntactic form.

As distant observers of the programs for ape language training, we have the impression that the initial high hopes of being able to communicate with apes at a human level have been disappointed. There seemed to be nothing of interest that the apes wanted to communicate. It was as if they had nothing equivalent to human thinking.

We agree with Karl Popper that human language at levels 3 and 4 of Figure 8-1 is outside the capacity of apes. The differences are qualitative. It would appear that there are special properties of the human brain not shared by other species. This gulf between animal and human linguistic performance must have been bridged nevertheless in the evolutionary process, but all intermediate forms such as *Homo habilis* and *Homo erectus* have died out. Presumably primitive human language at all the levels in Figure 8-1 was developed in the evolutionary climb of Homo sapiens.

Hominid Evolution

The last two decades have witnessed wonderful discoveries of hominid fossils in East Africa, particularly by the Leakeys. The most primitive hominid, *Australopithecus afarensis,* lived from 4 million to 2.5 million years ago and had an upright posture, but the brain was but little larger than for a pongid. In small, isolated breeding communities hominids with much larger brains (up to 770 ccm), *Homo habilis,* appeared about 2.5 million to 1.5 million years ago. Richard Leakey has now recovered several skulls in an amazing state of preservation. The later evolutionary development was to the still larger-brained (800 to 1,050 ccm) *Homo erectus* at 1.5 million to 500,000 years ago. They were widely scattered over Africa and Asia and had an advanced tool culture and the use of fire. Finally, through the stages of *Homo preneanderthalis, Homo sapiens neanderthalis* came to exist at 80,000 years ago with a brain averaging 1,400 ccm, at least as large as the present human brain (*Homo sapiens sapiens*). The successive stages of linguistic development and its relationship to brain development can never be known. It is, however, an attractive evolutionary hypothesis that brain development and speech development went hand in hand.

The higher levels of language probably have emerged in relation to the hunting and food-gathering of primitive hominids. The pragmatic level of ape language could have developed into more objective descriptions of the locations, numbers, and movements of prey, or there could have been descriptions of the locations and nature of edible fruits. With improvements in the descriptions there would be tests of their truth or falsity, so there could arise arguing, much as in children, and also the most important concepts of time and of the future. With this background in linguistic performance there eventually came the recognition of selfhood and of death. There is convincing evidence that this had occurred by the time Neanderthal man practiced ceremonial burial some 80,000 to 60,000 years ago. We can be confident that thought and language were well developed at that time as properties of the large brain, and at the same time there was an improvement of tool culture with designs having aesthetic appeal. We are at the onset of human personhood.

The Language Centers of the Human Brain

The three language centers of the brain are shown in Figure 8–2, located as they are in 95 percent of subjects in the left cerebral hemisphere. They were originally identified because of the disorders of language that resulted from their destruction. The posterior speech area, discovered by a young German neurologist named Wernicke, is specially associated with the ideational aspect of speech. There is a failure to understand speech, either written or spoken. Although the patient could speak with normal speed and rhythm, his speech was remarkably devoid of content, being a kind of nonsense jargon. Even earlier in the last century the French neurologist Broca discovered that with lesions of what we now call Broca's area the patient had lost the ability to speak, although he could understand spoken language. There were disorders in the use of the vocal musculature. The third speech area was recognized by Wilder Penfield on two grounds. First, stimulating it produced vocalization, but not recognizable speech. Second, removing it resulted in a temporary inability to speak of about two weeks' duration. It is now believed that recovery was due to the superior speech area of the other side, as will be described in Chapter 11. That is to say, the superior speech areas differ from the posterior and anterior in being bilateral.

As shown by studies of brain lesions in infants and children, both cerebral hemispheres participate in speech initially. Normally the left hemisphere gradually becomes dominant in speech performance, both in interpretation and in expression, presumably because of its superior neurological endowment. Meanwhile, the other hemis-

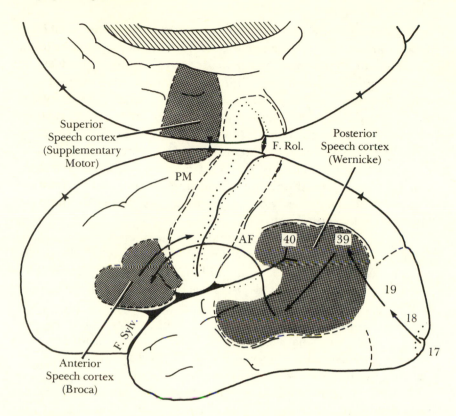

FIGURE 8–2. Cortical Speech Areas of the Dominant Left Hemisphere. Note that above the lateral view is the medial view of the left hemisphere, so that continuity from the convex surface to the medial surface can be appreciated. The pathway for reading aloud is shown by arrows from the visual areas of the cortex, the Brodmann areas 17, 18, 19, thence to the angular gyrus of the posterior speech area of Wernicke and so by the arcuate fasciculus, AF, to the anterior speech area of Broca and so to the motor cortex for speech production. Note also the superior speech area, which is identical with the supplementary motor area, which will be described in Chapter 11. F. Rol. is the fissure of Rolando, separating the motor cortex in front from the sensory cortex behind (cf. Figure 11–1).

phere, usually the right, is repressed in respect to speech production but retains some competence in understanding. This process of speech transfer is usually complete by four or five years of age.

As yet our understanding of the cerebral mechanisms of speech is at a very crude level. The arrows in Figure 8–2 show the neural pathways concerned in reading aloud. From the visual areas 17,18, and 19 the pathway is to area 19 (the angular gyrus). Lesions of area 19 result in dyslexia. At the next stage there is semantic interpretation by the Wernicke area, then transfer via the arcuate fasciculus (AF) to Broca's area for processing into the complex motor patterns required for activation of the motor cortex in order to give speech production.

Unfortunately, we are still quite ignorant of the detailed anatomical structures of the cortical speech areas that give them their unique properties. As mentioned above, there are functional speech areas in the right hemisphere for the first few years of life. Destruction of the speech areas in the left hemisphere results in full development of the linguistic function of the right hemisphere. During adolescence, however, this property of substitution is lost. All we can say is that some plastic property of the potential speech areas in the right hemisphere has atrophied.

It is important to recognize that the speech areas of the human brain are already formed before birth, being ontogenetically developed in readiness for the learning of language. This is a genetically coded process, and, amazingly, the speech areas so grown are competent for the learning of any human language. It has been established without doubt that children of different races are equipotent for any language. Chomsky has used this fact in formulating his ideas on the general principles of a universal grammar. Perhaps the deep structure of grammar can be homologized with the microorganization of the linguistic areas of the brain. In that sense it can be understood that a child is born with a "knowledge" of the deep structure of language because this is encoded in the microstructure of the linguistic areas of the cerebral cortex that genetic instructions have already caused to be built before birth.

Thought and the Brain

Early in this chapter we referred to the manner in which thoughts were expressed in language. We may inquire how the brain is concerned as an instrument in this transformation. A most important finding of Roger Sperry and associates was that when the two hemispheres were separated by commissurotomy, the patient suffered only a minor linguistic difficulty in expressing thoughts, because his self-conscious mind was operating through the linguistic areas of the left hemisphere in an apparently normal manner. By contrast the right hemisphere exhibited some understanding of written and spoken language but was extremely deficient in expression in speech or writing, which was effectively zero. However, it has been shown that the right hemisphere has the ability to recognize faces and even to display self-recognition. In general, therefore, because of the absence of the linguistic areas of the brain, the right hemisphere resembles in its performance the ape brain, though it is superior in language recognition. One can predict that, if trained by the methods used for teaching apes artificial language, the right hemisphere could learn more effectively than the apes. The left hand could be used to express in the artificial language techniques of Premack and Rumbaugh.

Thoughts in World 2 can be expressed in language via the speech areas of the left hemisphere, which is a particularly clear example of dualist-interactionism as diagrammed in Figure 3–1. This explanation is essentially that proposed by Descartes: that the self-conscious mind or soul gained expression in language by operation on the brain. However, we need not regard animals as automata in the Cartesian manner. They have conscious experiences (cf. Chapter 2), but it is doubtful how far even a chimpanzee has a recognition of self, Gallup's investigations notwithstanding. Since chimpanzees lack linguistic expressions except for their limited pragmatic communications, we may wonder how far they have any experiences corresponding to human thinking at the cognitive levels, 3 and 4, of language (Figure 8–1).

One feature of linguistic expression is rarely considered in depth. We can all recognize that when we are attempting to express subtle thoughts, particularly those that are novel and as yet unclear, we may tentatively try now this, now that verbal expression. In fact this is precisely what is done in writing this section. In attempting to convey some experience it is difficult to give satisfactory verbal expression to one's thoughts. One searches for the right words and syntactic arrangement so that one can have hope that one's thoughts may achieve a clear expression to listeners or readers.

How can we understand this creative act? We do so in terms of a dualist-interactionist hypothesis of the mind–brain problem, which is closely allied to the Cartesian theory of language given above. The subjectively experienced thoughts are initially in the mind (Figure 3–1, World 2). Expression in some verbal form comes when the mental events have brought about patterned operations in the speech areas of the brain, first the superior speech area (Figure 8–2), then Wernicke, then Broca, and so to overt expression in speaking or writing. These effects are World 1 events, but, as we have already seen above, thought expressions also have a World 3 status. There is a continuous ongoing judgment by the mind to see how far the expressed thoughts have been an acceptable World 3 display of the thought processes in World 2. Three comments may be made.

First, this evaluation can occur before there has been any overt expression. Sensitive speakers or writers judge verbal formulation as it appears in their self-consciousness. We can play with words in our mind before saying or writing anything, as we say, "before putting pen to paper." And this can occur even during an impromptu lecture. Our sentences seem to be generated just prior to utterance and momentarily can be subjected to some molding or can be immediately reexpressed in emended form. It all can happen to an experienced speaker as if by magic. Sometimes you can feel that you spoke better than you could have hoped! We are here immersed in the wonderful intensity and richness of mind–brain interaction. My hypothesis is that when thought processes achieve expression even in unspoken words, they have been transferred to patterned operation of the neural machinery first in the SMA (Figure 8–2). Yet we in World 2, as conscious evaluators of our linguistic performances, stand outside the brain events in World 1 and their expression in World 3. We can now begin to appreciate the wonder and mystery of great creative writing, for example, how the thoughts of John Keats came to be immortalized in his odes. Materialists must fail completely to recognize and appreciate the sublime performance of a creative genius. They can do so only by "putting on another hat"!

Second, from the effort of expression we can achieve a clarity of understanding of what was heretofore obscure. A teacher should ask students to write out their thoughts or to convert them into a diagram. They may fail, but if they succeed they will have learned much, and there is now a World 3 object that can be criticized.

Third, we have ideas in the mind that have no relationship to linguistic expression and may never be expressed. For example, think of the visual and auditory experiences crowding in as one walks alone along a country path. Some behaviorists make the absurd claim that such experiences depend on silent utterances. How could you utter the experience of a tree in all of its branching complexity? The fact is that we have whole ranges of experiences unrelated to verbal expressions, as is immediately evident when we think of a musician or of a pictorial artist. In later life Gilbert Ryle became troubled by the stark behaviorist doctrine expressed in his *Concept of Mind*. In his posthumous publication there is an account of how he envisages thoughts that can exist without an expression in behavior, verbal or otherwise.

At the highest level of conscious experience we can have an extraordinarily varied range of thoughts, often with intense emotional tuning: feelings of enjoyment or of contentment or of understanding; a numinous feeling of wonder and worship; thoughts of delight in beauty and loveliness in nature, literature, music, art and in fellow beings. But experiences can also be somber or terrifying. There can be loneliness, melancholy, anxiety, fear, or terror. We suggest that these experiences in the mind (World 2) need not have a neuronal counterpart in brain activity (World 1). Of course, transformation into brain activity occurs as soon as we try to define such experiences clearly for expression in some linguistic mode or other behavior. Then there will be reciprocal communication across the frontier in Figure 3–1, particularly when the expression is being subjected to self-critical judgment.

Language and Human Thought: A Reappraisal

In the bulk of this chapter we have given every benefit of the doubt to theorists and researchers who have defended the continuity thesis of linguistic and cognitive prowess. Our modest conclusion to this point has been that even the apes have failed to attain the level of linguistic and cognitive performance common to the human species, though the apes do give evidence of a primordial version of both.

There is, however, a more radical conclusion, no less defensible for being radical. It may be argued that in *none* of the studies involving "language training" of nonhuman organisms is there *any* evidence whatever of *linguistic* competence, taking language in the sense of the Bühler-Popper levels 3 and 4 (Figure 8–1). Support for this thesis arises from two broad considerations: First, every example of "language learning" *can* be explained as no more than and no different from the sort of sequential, discriminative behavior easily acquired by rats, pigeons, and other nonprimates through the intricacies of operant (Skinnerian) conditioning. Second, every "symbol" acquired by the trained apes is a *denotatum* that refers to a specific physical stimulus or array of stimuli. None of the symbols is connotative or is used connotatively. That is, in none of the behavior thus studied and reported is there any evidence of *abstraction* and the representation (symbolization) of abstract concepts. In light of this, it is entirely warranted, if argumentative, to suggest that in all of this work *language* hasn't been studied at all! Both of these considerations are worth amplifying.

It is very much to the credit of B. F. Skinner and his disciples to have illustrated the extraordinary range of behavior that can be brought about by the appropriate manipulation of the animal's immediate environment. By varying the intervals between successive rewards and by varying the ratio of responses to rewards it is possible to "shape" behavior in a way that remains stable over weeks or even months. Similarly, the behavior can be stretched into long chains of responses such as those emitted by the famous Columbia University rat Barnabas, who would climb scaffolds, row little boats, and otherwise solve a wide variety of problems in order to obtain a pellet of food.

Even the (cerebrally) lowly pigeon can be conditioned to peck at specific patterns of stimuli presented within a very complex background array and to do so at a desired rate and in nearly any desired order.

When a Washoe, a Lana, or a Sarah is taught what is, in question-begging fashion, called a *language*—whether this is American Sign Language or the manipulation of certain objects in a given sequence—the actual conditioned *behavior* takes the form of sequences of responses tied to specific external stimuli. Let us recall the example given in Chapter 5 where Lana is said to signal something like

DON . . . GIVE LANA WATER

What a chimpanzee has actually done is press a set of keys in a specific order. It was, after all, Dr. Rumbaugh and his colleagues who decided that one key-panel was "DON," another "GIVE," another "LANA," and another "WATER." Suppose we inscribe on the DON key a cube; on the GIVE key a pyramid; on the LANA key a cylinder; on the WATER key a sphere. Now, however, instead of using a chimpanzee we select a pigeon and, through successive reinforcements, make the availability of water contingent on the bird's pecking at pictures of these symbols in the fixed order, DON-GIVE-LANA-WATER. Now, the average laboratory pigeon will acquire such a chain in a matter of a week or two. After this has occurred, we bring a stranger into the laboratory and declare that we have a "linguistic" pigeon who "asks for water." Sure enough, once the demonstration begins, the bird faces a screen containing, say, three hundred symbols, and immediately pecks only the four associated with the delivery of a water reinforcement. In time the same pigeon would no doubt "ask for" food, warmth, the cessation of shock, illumination, perhaps even a mate.

It is important to make this point using pigeons, for here we have a member of a species whose cortical endowment is aptly captured by the epithet "birdbrain"! Recall that the chief argument to the effect that chimpanzees *ought* to be able to learn a language is that their brains are (somehow) very much "like" ours. But if their allegedly linguistic performance can be nearly matched by birds, the argument from (anatomical) analogy simply collapses.

Let us turn now to the second point, that pertaining to the connotative nature and functions of language. *Thought* is not just knowledge and memory by another name. If all that thought implied was the revival of past perceptions, the word "memory" would be one of its synonyms.

When Descartes looked for the basis on which a well-designed and cleverly constructed machine would fail to be confused with a human being, he arrived at three criteria: No machine would ever attain to the idea of God, would ever engage in *abstract* thought, or would ever engage *creatively* in language. Actually, all three of these criteria can be melded into the single criterion of *abstract thought.* What Descartes had in mind was the thought enlisted by logical and mathematical propositions and by certain nonphysical (but consciously real) entities such as morals, justice, virtue, and truth. Any machine, no matter how complex, must be no more than a collection of physical *parts,* which, as such, can be affected only by physical *things.* A device of this kind could record external events, could move in conformity with external forces and impositions, and so on. We might say that such a device could display what we often take to be evidence of learning, memory, even perception. Surely such a device could emit something like DON-GIVE-LANA-WATER when its water tanks ran low. But what such a device could not do is demand justice or fairness; it could have no allegiance and suffer no guilt; it could not have faith in the unseen nor could it know *itself,* even as it recited the list of its parts. Picking up on what was developed in Chapter 3, we can say that such a device could have no knowledge of a *self,* for this too is an abstract concept. Just as *every* feature of our own material bodies constantly undergoes change, so too must every feature of the device's material body. Thus, *self* as a unified and enduring entity would be represented by *nothing* to which the device could be made sensitive.

If we take evolutionary theory to be the last word on human personhood, then of course we must expect every human attribute to have its ancestry in the animal kingdom. We must therefore be *sur-*

prised to discover that, for example, only we have language at the two higher levels shown in Figure 8–1, and the balance of cognitive prowess that language confers. But this is all treasonous to the very character of scientific integrity and impartiality. What the impartial scientist demands is that every theoretical proposition be tested against the observable facts of nature. If the proposition fails the test, it must be modified; where it resists modification, it must be abandoned.

Human persons unequivocally have the gift of language (Figure 6–1), which is defined as the ability to symbolize (denote) objects, to communicate concepts, and to arrange such symbols and communications in combinations of infinite variety according to grammatical rules. In possession of this gift, the human species is able to structure the material world according to principles which themselves are immaterial but utterly compatible with and needed by the transcendent nature of the human person. This structure, in its most developed form, contains the ingredients of *culture,* itself intelligible only at the level of cognitive abstraction—World 3.

Needless to say, the reservations Descartes had regarding the mechanical device's capacity for abstraction must extend to any entity that is purely material. In this respect it would be hazardous to think even of the human brain as ''engaged in abstract thought'' or as ''engaged in language.'' It is enough for persons of common sense to respect the fact that *persons* are thus engaged and that, to do so, persons make use of their brains (cf. Figure 3–1). But to take all of the established attributes of persons—attributes that have been forthcoming only from persons—and assign them to *any* material entity, including the brain, is to leave the arena of science and enter that of superstition.

It is also important to emphasize that the facts of human language cannot be explained merely by noting our exceptional capacities of learning and memory, the subject of the next chapter. That is, a *behavioristic* explanation of language by now has proved to be notoriously defective. What any such explanation must finally come to rely on is some sort of associative, trial-and-error process to which practice and rewards are essential. But only a few facts are sufficient to raise the gravest doubts about such an account:

1. Children the world over come to engage in *grammatical* speech at very nearly the same ages, despite the widest variations in childrearing and in attention to language development.
2. Parents are famously indifferent to the *grammar* of the child's utterances and nearly universally confine rewards to the

specific *content* of such utterances. Nonetheless, the child displays just this grammar, largely in defiance of the "law" of reinforcement.

3. Children reared in linguistically impoverished environments (e.g. by deaf-mute parents in rustic isolation) come to attain normal or very nearly normal linguistic abilities extremely quickly when transferred to linguistically nurturing settings. The speed with which language then appears makes it quite evident that a merely associative, trial-and-error process is of secondary importance.

4. Children comprehend and obey linguistic utterances well before they can articulate them themselves. There is, then, a knowledge of language quite apart from the (behavioral) use or expression of it.

5. Persons can understand and can articulate a veritable *infinity* of grammatically correct sentences in their native language. This domain is simply too large to be explained as the result of rewarded practice.

6. The child—a "developing linguist"—does not first speak a poor or an erroneous version of adult language, but a child language containing specific rules and structures. The adult language *replaces* this and is not merely a corrected version of it.

The behavioristic account turns out to be an explanation at most of the means by which we come to possess specific *words,* but not an explanation of language *qua* language. The analogy of the adding machine might clarify the distinction. An adding machine is a device constructed in such a way that if we succeed in getting items into it, the items will be added; that is, the items will be processed according to fixed rules, in this case the rules of arithmetic. We might say, then, that trial-and-error learning and rewarded practice are the means by which words are entered into the linguistic system. But it is the design features of the system that determine how these "inputs" will be processed. The rules and formal structures that give language its defining character are all internal and must be assumed if language is to appear at all. The human brain possesses the necessary complexity and interconnectedness by which to represent such rules and formal structures. Thus is the person able to use the brain as the essential tool in the forging of adult language and the thought this language permits.

Suggested Readings

BROWN, R. *A first language: The early stages.* Cambridge, Mass.: Harvard University Press, 1973.

CHOMSKY, N. *Reflections on language.* New York: Pantheon, 1975.

ECCLES, J. C. *The understanding of the brain.* New York: McGraw-Hill, 1973, Ch. 6.

ECCLES, J. C. *The human mystery.* Berlin, Heidelberg, New York: Springer Verlag Internat., 1979, Chs. 5, 6.

ECCLES, J. C. *The human psyche.* Berlin, Heidelberg, New York: Springer Verlag Internat., 1980, Chs. 1,7.

GESCHWIND, N. Language and the brain. *Sci. Amer.*, 1972, *226* (4), 76–83.

LENNEBERG, E. H. On explaining language. *Science,* 1969, *164,* 635–643.

PENFIELD, W. *The mystery of the mind.* Princeton, N.J.: Princeton University Press, 1975.

PENFIELD, W., and ROBERTS, L. *Speech and brain-mechanisms.* Princeton, N.J.: Princeton University Press, 1959.

POPPER, K. R., and ECCLES, J. C. *The self and its brain.* Berlin, Heidelberg, New York: Springer Verlag Internat., 1977, Chs. P3, E4, Dialogues III,V.

SEBEOK, T. A., and UMIKER-SEBEOK, D. J. *Speaking of apes.* New York: Plenum Press, 1980.

SPERRY, R. *Science and moral priority.* New York: Columbia University Press, 1983.

9

Learning and Memory

Without memory there could be no knowing of existence. It links our moment-to-moment experiences into a strand extending backward in time to give that existential unity which is the self each of us knows. Without conscious memory we could not know of the human mystery. Without memory we would just be reacting from moment to moment according to the input from the environment in a standard, stereotyped way, like the unthinking behavior of fish, for example. There could be no human personhood.

There is no more wonderful and necessary function of the brain than its ability *to learn* and to retrieve what is learned in the *memory process*. For each of us the most precious activities throughout our lifetime involve the storage of experiences, which in this way are made uniquely ours in that they are available for our *reenactment* or *recall* in the memory process. These two words are chosen because there are two main kinds of learning and memory, though in many situations they are closely linked together. *First* is motor learning and memory, which is the learning of all skilled movements. The repertoire is immense: the playing of all musical instruments and games, as well as the learning of all arts, crafts, and technologies. Furthermore, there are all the expressive movements, as in speaking, dancing, caressing,

125

singing, drawing, and writing. *Second* is what we may call cognitive learning and memory. At the simplest level there is the ability to recall some perceptual experience, but all levels can be involved, e.g. the remembrance of faces, names, scenes, events, pictures, musical themes. Then at a higher level there is the learning of language, stories, and the contents of disciplines from the simplest technologies through the most refined academic studies in the humanities and in the sciences.

It is a familiar observation that there may be an enduring cognitive memory of some single highly emotional experience. We now recognize that this endurance is due to the continued recall of this experience. We often say that we "could not get it out of our mind for days." On the other hand, motor memories require reinforcement by continual practice if they are to be retained at a high level of skill. Quite distinct parts of the brain are concerned in these two types of memory. Nevertheless, it appears likely that the same kinds of neural mechanisms are concerned.

In the last three decades great progress has been made in the understanding of many activities of the brain both at the elemental level, such as the propagation of nerve impulses in nerve fibers and the generation of these impulses by synaptic action on neurons, and at more complex levels, such as the operation of neuronal pathways concerned in the many sensory systems and in the motor system as described in Chapter 11. In all of these fields there is a large measure of agreement. By contrast, there have been many divergent and even irreconcilable views on the nature of the neuronal mechanisms concerned in learning and memory. But in the last few years the situation has changed dramatically. We now have an excellent neuronal model for memory in the hippocampus, a primitive part of the cerebral cortex lying deep in the temporal lobe. That story will be presented in the section headed "Neural Pathways Concerned in Laying Down Long-term Memories." I shall confine my story to cognitive memory in the widest sense, because it is of particular significance to the human mystery and also because it is possible to build up this story from observations on human subjects with only passing reference to experiments on nonhuman primates.

I shall attempt to answer the question: How can we recover or reexperience some events or some simple test situation, as for example a number or word sequence? It will be recognized that two distinct problems are involved: storage and retrieval or, in relation to our present problem of conscious memory, learning and remembering. I propose to deal with these problems at two levels.

First it will be considered as a problem of neurobiology, namely the structural and functional changes that form the basis of memory. It is generally supposed that the recall of a memory involves the replay in an approximate manner of the neuronal events that were originally responsible for the experience being recalled. There is no specially difficult problem with short-term memories (for a few seconds). It can be conjectured that this is effected by the neural events continuing during the verbal or pictorial rehearsal. The distinctive patterns of modular activity suggested in Chapter 3 thus continue to recirculate for the whole duration of these brief memories and are available for readout. On the other hand, with memories enduring for minutes to years, it has to be discovered how the neuronal connectivities are changed so that there tends to be stabilized some tendency for replay of the spatiotemporal patterns of modular activity that occurred in the initial experience, and that have meanwhile subsided.

Second, with cognitive memories the role of the self-conscious mind has to be considered. It was conjectured in Chapter 3 that a conscious experience arises when the self-conscious mind enters into an effective relationship with certain activated modules, "open" modules, in the cerebral cortex (Figure 3–1). In the willed recall of a memory the self-conscious mind must again be in relationship to a pattern of modular responses resembling the original responses evoked by the event to be remembered, so that there is a reading out of approximately the same experience. We have to consider how the self-conscious mind is concerned in calling forth the modular events that give the remembered experience on demand, as it were. Futhermore, the self-conscious mind acts as an arbiter or assessor with respect to the correctness or relevance of the memory that is delivered on demand. For example, the name or number may be recognized as incorrect by the self-conscious mind, and a further recall process may be instituted, and so on. Thus the recall of a memory involves two distinct processes in the self-conscious mind; first, that of initiating a recall from the data banks in the brain, and second, the recognition memory that judges its correctness.

Role of the Self-conscious Mind in Short-term Memory

Let us consider some simple and unique perceptual experience, for example, the first sight of a bird or flower hitherto unknown to us or of a new model of a car. First come the many stages of encoded transmission from retinal image to the various levels of the visual cortex. At a further stage we propose the activation of modules of the liaison brain that are "open" to World 2 and the consequent readout by the self-conscious mind, giving the perceptual experience with all its sensual richness. This read-out by the self-conscious mind involves the integration into a unified experience of the specific activities of many modules (cf. Chapter 3), an integration that gives pictured uniqueness to the experience. Furthermore, it is a two-way action, the self-conscious mind modifying the modular activity as well as receiving from it (cf. the reciprocal arrows in Figure 3–1), and possibly evaluating it by testing procedures in an input–output manner. Moreover, we have to postulate closed self-reexciting chains of nerve cells in these ongoing patterns of modular interaction. In this way there is a continuation of the dynamic patterned activity in time.

As long as the modular activities continue in this specific patterned interaction, we assume that the self-conscious mind is continuously able to read it out according to its interests and attention. We may say that in this way the new experience is kept in mind, as, for example, when we try to remember a telephone number during the time between looking it up and dialing.

We propose that the continued activity of the modules can be secured by continuous active intervention or reinforcement by the self-conscious mind (cf. Figure 3–1), which in this way can hold memories by processes that we experience and refer to as either verbal or nonverbal (pictorial or musical, for example) rehearsal. As soon as the self-conscious mind engages in some other task, this reinforcement ceases, that specific pattern of neuronal activities subsides, and the short-term memory is lost. Recall now becomes dependent on memory processes of longer duration.

Neural Pathways Concerned in Laying Down Long-term Memories

In general terms, following Tanzi, Ramón y Cajal, Sherrington, Adrian, Hebb, and Szentágothai, we have to suppose that long-term memories are somehow encoded in the neuronal connectivities of the brain. We are thus led to conjecture that the structural basis of memory lies in the enduring modifications of synapses, which are the functional connections between nerve cells. In mammals there is no evidence for growth or change of major neuronal pathways in the brain after their initial formation. It is not possible to construct or reconstruct major brain pathways at such a gross level. But it should be possible to secure the necessary changes in neuronal connectivity by microstructural changes in synapses. For example, they may be hypertrophied for storing a memory, as is shown diagrammatically in Figure 9–1 for spine synapses on a dendritic branch of a nerve cell, and in forgetting they may regress. It would be expected that the increased synaptic efficacy would arise because of a strong conditioning synaptic activation, and this potentiation has been shown to occur and even to continue for weeks with several types of synapses in the brain, particularly in the primitive part of the cerebral cortex called the hippocampus.*

Physiological experiments have indicated that the modifiable synapses which could be responsible for memory are excitatory and are specially prominent at the higher levels of the brain. In the cerebral cortex the great majority of excitatory synapses on pyramidal cells are on their dendritic spines, as is indicated in Figure 9–1, one being shown in detail in the upper inset. It is conjectured that these spine synapses on the dendrites of such neurons as the pyramidal cells of the cerebral cortex and the hippocampus are the modifiable synapses concerned in learning. These would be the synapses displaying the indefinitely prolonged potentiation required for long-term memory. One can imagine that the superior performance by these synapses was indefinitely prolonged because a growth process had developed in the dendritic spines, giving a structural change which could have great endurance. Moreover, there is now a convincing demonstration in electron micrographs by Eva Fifková and associates that this growth of activated spine synapses on hippocampal granule cells does occur.

The factors concerned in the memory process of the hippocampus have undergone intensive study. On the basis of these studies the hypothesis was developed that the strong and enduring synaptic stimulation for effecting the prolonged changes required for memory is brought about by calcium influx into the dendrites. The calcium combines with a recently discovered protein, calmodulin, to form a complex having a powerful metabolic action with manufacture of proteins and other macromolecules required for a permanent increase in the synaptic potency. This leads to the immense new field of

*The hippocampus is located deep in the temporal lobe, about 6 cm in from the junction of the ear with the scalp.

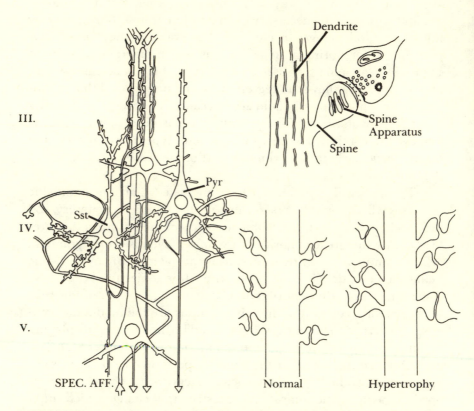

FIGURE 9–1. Drawing of Four Neurons of the Cerebral Cortex. This shows the excitatory synaptic connections set up by an input fiber from the thalamus labeled (spec. aff.), which is an enormous nucleus in the brain that provides the principal inputs to the cerebral cortex. This spec. aff. fiber branches profusely to make excitatory synapses on the spiny stellate cell (Sst) and on one pyramidal cell (Pyr). All three pyramidal cells receive on their spines excitatory synapses from Sst, and there is a special excitatory structure, called by Szentágothai a cartridge, formed by the synaptic endings on the apical dendrites of two pyramidal cells. All three pyramidal cells, but not the Sst, send their axons out of the cerebral cortex as shown by the lower projecting arrows. The upper inset shows an enlargement of a spine synapse with synaptic vesicles in the presynaptic ending and the spine arising from a dendrite. The lower two insets show diagrammatically normal and hypertrophied spine synapses. [Principal figure from Szentágothai, 1978.]

neurochemistry, which is beyond our scope in this general account of long-term memory.

Loss of Long-term Memory
After Hippocampectomy

A fruitful approach to the problem of long-term memory is to study the brains of patients who have lost their ability to store new memories. The damaged regions in the brains of these amnesic patients should give clues to the areas of the brain involved in memory storage.

The clinical condition that is distinctively characterized by loss of memory, amnesia, is usually called Korsakoff's syndrome after its discoverer, who first described it in 1887. Such patients have good memories for their experiences before the onset of the disease and also memories for happenings in the previous few seconds, the short-term memory dealt with above. In ordinary conversation they may not noticeably disclose their disability. However, they fail in the retention of memory as soon as they are distracted by a new situation. For example, a convenient clinical test is to ask the patient to remember simple bits of information such as the name of the doctor, the date, and the time of day. The patient fails in such a test even though under instruction just before he had repeated the answers hundreds of times. But of course the defect applies to every new experience of the patient. He fails to remember names, objects, events—in fact anything he reads or sees or hears. However, memory for the remote past, years before the onset of the disease, is well retained. Nevertheless, the well-remembered past is not sharply separated from the later amnestic period. In between are fragmentary memories that often are given incorrect time sequences and with varying degrees of inaccuracy. Strangely, the patients fail to realize the severity of their memory defect or even its existence. Often it is covered up by confabulation in which the patient invents experiences and happenings. For example, a bedridden patient may assert that he has just come back from a walk in the garden and give a description of his experiences there!

The classic amnesic syndrome as described by Korsakoff was due to alcoholism, but it is now recognized that it may be caused by many other illnesses. Perhaps the most frequent cases of memory defects of varying degrees of severity are the results of senile dementia and of Alzheimer's Syndrome, now being recognized as a major hazard of old age. Unfortunately, there is such a wide dispersal of the degenerated areas and such variability from one patient to another that no clear picture emerges of the cerebral regions involved in learning and memory. The much more sharply defined lesions produced by surgical excisions would be of inestimable value, and it is to these that we now turn.

Remarkable evidence has been found, particularly by Brenda Milner, in support of the concept that the hippocampus plays a key role in human cognitive memory. It may arouse skepticism when we state that the really convincing evidence comes from investigations on one patient (H.M.), who in 1953 was subjected to an operative excision bilaterally of the hippocampus and the adjacent medial temporal lobe. The operation was designed to alleviate epileptic seizures of incapacitating severity that were uncontrolled by maximum anticonvulsant medication. Therapeutically the operation was a success in alleviating the seizures, but it produced an extreme amnesic syndrome resembling Korsakoff's syndrome, only more severe. This operation of course will never be carried out again, so H.M. and three others will remain unique cases for all time.

Despite his grave amnesia H.M. is a remarkably tolerant and cooperative person with fairly good intelligence. In fact he has been an ideal subject for investigation for nearly thirty years, being perhaps more intensively investigated than any other neurological patient in history. Let us now look at some of the findings on this unique patient. H.M. lives entirely with short-term memories of a few seconds' duration and with the memories retained from before the operation. Milner gives a graphic account of his memory loss:

> His mother observes that he will do the same jigsaw puzzle day after day without showing any practice effect and read the same magazines over and over without ever finding their contents familiar. The same forgetfulness applies to people he has met since the operation. His initial emotional reaction may be intense, but it will be short-lived, since the incident provoking it is soon forgotten. Thus, when informed of the death of his uncle, of whom he was very fond, he became extremely upset, but then appeared to forget the whole matter and from time to time thereafter would ask when his uncle was coming to visit them; each time on hearing anew of the uncle's death, he would show the same intense dismay, with no sign of habituation.

He can keep current events in mind so long as he is not distracted. For example, he has succeeded in remembering a three-figure number sequence, such as 5, 8, 4, for as long as fifteen minutes by continually repeating it to himself. But distraction completely eliminates all trace of what he has been doing only a few seconds before. H.M. provides a unique example of short-term memory in its purest form. The only way in which this patient can hold on to new information is by constant verbal rehearsal, and forgetting occurs as soon as this rehearsal is prevented by some new activity claiming his attention.

There are three other recorded cases where a comparable severe anterograde amnesia (amnesia for all happenings after the operation) resulted from destruction of both hippocampi. There is no obvious impairment of intellect or personality in these subjects despite the acute failure of memory. In fact, they live either in the immediate present or with remembered experiences from before the time of the operation. It has been shown by a testing procedure of prompting that a minimal storage of pictorial information even occurs for experiences after the operation, but it is of no use to the patient, because he cannot himself provide the prompting.

There is a limited amnesia following unilateral hippocampectomy—for words and numbers with the left and for patterns and shapes with the right—but, as this is not unduly incapacitating, this operation is frequently performed. However, it is essential to discover if the other hippocampus is normal.

The Location of Memory Storage

Three concepts of the hippocampal role in memory storage have been formulated by Hans Kornhüber. (1) In retrieving the memory of an event that is not being continuously rehearsed in the short-term memory process, the self-conscious mind is dependent on some consolidation or storage process that is brought about by hippocampal activity. (2) The hippocampus itself is not the site of the storage. (3) We conjecture that the hippocampal participation in the consolidation process is dependent on neuronal pathways that transmit from the modules of the association cortex to the hippocampus and thence back to the frontal lobe.

The role of the hippocampus in memory consolidation is illustrated schematically in Figure 9–2. All of the pathways shown in this block diagram have been anatomically identified. Each of the pathways is constituted by hundreds of thousands or even millions of nerve

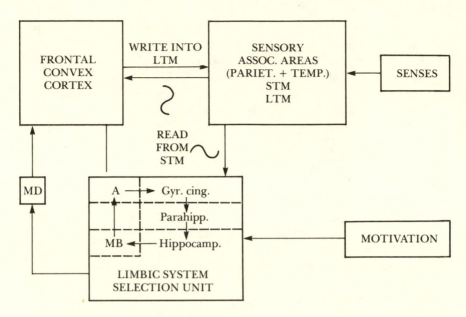

FIGURE 9-2. Diagram Drawn by Hans Kornhüber to Illustrate the Circuits Involved in Laying Down Long-term Memories. The diagram shows the sensory inputs to the sensory cortical areas as in Figure 11-1 and the two circuits from there to the frontal cortex as described in the text, one direct by association pathways of the cerebral cortex, the other indirect by the hippocampus.

fibers. To the upper right is a sensory input to the primary sensory areas for vision, hearing, and touch in Figure 9-1, and then there is transmission in the conventional manner to the many sensory association areas, particularly in the parietal and temporal lobes. At that stage there is bifurcation, there being an association pathway to the frontal cortex and a path down to the hippocampus. The hippocampal output is shown partly going to the frontal cortex via the medial dorsal (MD) thalamus and partly in a local loop, MB → A → Gyr.cing. → Hippocampus, the so-called Papez loop.

Thus in Figure 9-2 two pathways are shown converging on the frontal cortex: that from the sensory association areas directly, and that indirectly via a detour through the hippocampus and MD thalamus. In the frontal cortex this input from MD would be exciting the spiny stellate cells (Sst in Figure 9-1), and so to the cartridge type of synapse on the apical dendrites of the pyramidal cell that is also shown in figure 9-3. On the other hand, the direct input would be by association (ASS) and commissural (COM) fibers, which can be seen in Figure 9-3 bifurcating to form the horizontal fibers that make syn-

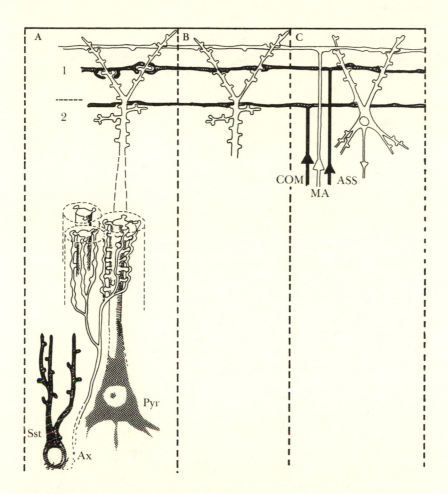

FIGURE 9-3. Simplified Diagram of Connectivities in the Neocortex. Diagram is constructed in order to show pathways and synapses in the proposed theory of cerebral learning. The diagram shows three modules, A, B, C. In laminae I and II are horizontal fibers arising as bifurcating axons of commissural (COM) and association (ASS) fibers and also of Martinotti axons (MA) from module C. The horizontal fibers make synapses with the apical dendrites of the stellate pyramidal cell in module C and of pyramidal cells in modules A and B. Deeper is shown a spiny stellate cell (Sst) with axon (Ax) making cartridge synapses with the shafts of apical dendrites of pyramidal cells (Pyr). Because of conjunction, as described in the text, there has been a selective hypertrophy of synapses formed by the horizontal ASS fibers on the apical dendrites of the pyramidal cell in module A, but not on that of module B.

aptic contacts with the spine synapses on the apical dendrites of the pyramidal cells.

It is proposed that the cartridge-type synapse exerts such a powerful synaptic activation that it causes the influx of calcium ions, as described earlier, so producing long-term potentiation of the activated synapses. At the same time some impulses from the sensory association cortex (Figure 9–2) would be synaptically acting on the apical dendrites by the horizontal fibers (Figure 9–3), there being about two thousand such synapses on each pyramidal cell. Those few horizontal fiber synapses activated at the same time as the cartridge activation would participate in the long-term potentiation induced by the calcium influx. Thus a selection occurs on the basis of temporal conjunction in the manner originally proposed by David Marr. It is proposed that this highly selective potentiation forms the basis of memory storage in the cerebral cortex. The whole operation is too intricate for description in this book. All we give is the outline of the first clear story of the synaptic events in memory and of the key role of the hippocampus. This hypothesis will be a great challenge.

We are all cognizant that we do not store as memories experiences that are of no interest to us and to which we pay no attention. On the other hand, the familiar statement that a single sharp experience is remembered for a lifetime overlooks the fact that the intense emotional involvement is reexperienced incessantly immediately after the original, highly charged emotional experience. Evidently there has been a long series of ''replays'' of the patterns of cortical activity associated with the original experience, and this activity would particularly involve the hippocampal system as indicated by the strong emotional overtones. Thus there must be built into the neuronal machinery of the cortex and the Papez circuit of the hippocampus (Figure 9–2) the propensity for the reverberating circuit activity which would cause the synaptic potentiation giving the memory. In the further development of our hypothesis of long-term conscious memory we would propose that the self-conscious mind would enter into this transaction between the modules of the liaison brain (Figure 3–1) and the hippocampus in two ways: first, in keeping up the modular activity by the general action of interest or attention (the motivation system of Kornhüber, Figure 9–2), so that the hippocampal circuit of Figure 9–2 would be continuously reinforced; and second, in a more concentrated manner by probing into the appropriate modules to read out their storage and if necessary to reinforce it or modify it by direct action on the modules concerned. Both of these proposed actions are from the self-conscious mind to those modules that have the special property of being open to it (cf. Figure 3-1).

Memory Retrieval

It can be conjectured that literally millions of neurons participate in building up the specific pattern or engram that gives some particular memory to the mind. According to the generally accepted growth theory of learning—and its more precisely formulated hypothesis here presented—synapses are selectively potentiated by activity. Thus some particular spatiotemporal pattern of neuronal activity comes to be stabilized by usage so that at some later time it can be caused to be replayed in the neuronal "machinery" of the cortex and thus remembered in the mind. It is essential to recognize that any particular neuron or modular assemblage of neurons can participate in a virtually infinite variety of spatiotemporal patterns, and hence of potential memories. The idea of one memory for a neuron or a particular neuronal assembly (a module) has been rendered obsolete by our great progress in scientific understanding of the cerebral cortex.

In retrieval of a memory we have further to conjecture that the self-conscious mind is continuously searching to recover memories, e.g. words, phrases, sentences, ideas, events, pictures, and melodies, by actively scanning through the modular array of the cerebral cortex, which is so inadequately represented in Figure 3-1, and that, by its action on the preferred active modules, it tries to evoke the full neural patterned operation that it can read out as a recognizable memory rich in emotional and/or intellectual and cognitive content. Largely this could be by a trial-and-error process. We are familiar with the ease or difficulty of recall of one or another memory and of the strategies we learn in order to recover memories of names that for some unknown reason are refractory to recall. We can imagine that our self-conscious mind is under a continual challenge to recall the desired memory by discovering the appropriate entry into module operation that would by development give the appropriate patterned array of modules. Even in a simple memory recall there probably would be hundreds of modules to be initially selected in defining the specificity of the memory together with thousands of modules in the response that delivers the fully fashioned memory by virtue of some specific spatiotemporal pattern of activity—the data bank analogy.

It is proposed that there are two distinct kinds of conscious memory. Data bank memory is stored in the brain, and its retrieval from the brain is often by a deliberate mental act. Then another memory process comes into play, what we may call recognition memory. The retrieval from the data banks is critically scrutinized in the mind. It may be judged erroneous—perhaps a slight error in a name or in a number sequence. This leads to a renewed attempt at retrieval, which may again be judged faulty, and so on until the retrieval is judged to be correct or until the attempt is abandoned. It is therefore conjectured that there are two distinct kinds of memory: (1) brain storage memory held in the data banks of the brain, especially in the cerebral cortex, and (2) recognition memory, applied by the self-conscious mind in its scrutiny of the retrievals from the brain storage memories. There is further discussion of memory retrieval in recent books by Popper and Eccles and by Eccles.

Wilder Penfield gave a most illuminating account of the experiential responses evoked in fifty-three patients by stimulation of the cerebral cortex during operations performed under local anaesthesia. These responses differed from those produced by stimulation of the primary sensory areas (cf. Figure 11–1), which were merely flashes of light or touches and paraesthesia, in that the patients had experiences that resembled dreams. During the continued gentle electrical stimulation of sites on the exposed surface of their brains, the patients reported experiences that they often recognized as recalls of long-forgotten memories. As Penfield states, it is as if a past stream of consciousness is recovered during this electrical stimulation. The most common experiences were visual or auditory, but there were also many cases combining the visual and the auditory. The recall of music and song provided very striking experiences for both the patient and the neurosurgeon. All these results were obtained from brains of patients with a history of epileptic seizures. It is noteworthy that the temporal lobes were the preferred sites for stimulation and that the minor hemisphere was more effective than the dominant speech hemisphere (cf. Chapter 3). The primary sensory areas (cf. Figure 11–1) are excluded. In the summary of these most interesting investigations it is stated that the experiences are those in which the patient is an observer and not a participator, just as in dreams. The times summoned up most frequently are occasions of watching or hearing the action and speech of others and of hearing music.

It can be concluded that the stimulation acts as a mode of recall of past experiences. We may regard this as an instrumental means for a recovery of memories. It can be suggested that the storage of these memories is likely to be in cerebral areas close to the effective stimulation sites. It is important to recognize, however, that the experiential recall is evoked from areas in the region of the disordered cerebral function that is displayed by the epileptic seizures. Conceivably the effective sites are abnormal zones that are thereby able to act by association pathways to the much wider areas of the cerebral cortex, which are the actual storage sites for the memories.

Duration of Memories

An analysis of the durations of the various processes involved in memory provides evidence for two distinct memory processes. We have already presented evidence for the short-term memory, usually of a few seconds, which can be attributed to the continual activity in neural circuits, which holds the memory in a dynamic pattern of circulating impulses. The patients with bilateral hippocampectomy have almost no other memory. Secondly, there is the long-term memory, which endures for days to years. According to the growth theory of learning, this memory (or memory trace) is encoded in the increased efficacy of synapses that have been hypertrophied by conjunction with hippocampal inputs (Figure 9–3). In the present context of conscious memory it can be conjectured that this synaptic growth would occur in multitudes of synapses in patterned array in the modules strongly reacting in response to the original episode that sets in train the operation of the reverberatory circuits through the hippocampus. As a consequence of this synaptic growth, the self-conscious mind would be able to develop strategies for causing the replay of modules in a pattern resembling that of the original episode, hence the memory experience. This replay would be accompanied, however, by a renewed reverberatory activity through the hippocampus resembling the original, with a consequent strengthening of the memory trace.

Retrograde Amnesia

It is a common observation that loss of memory results from a severe trauma of the brain, as for example from mechanical damage causing unconsciousness (concussion), or from the convulsive seizures occurring in electroshock therapy. The retrograde amnesia is usually complete for events immediately before the trauma and becomes progressively less severe for memories of earlier and still earlier events. Depending on the severity of the trauma, retrograde amnesia may cover periods of minutes, hours, or days.

Following hippocampectomy there was not only the severe anterograde amnesia already described for events following the operation but also a severe retrograde amnesia, that is, for events preceding the operation by days. Apparently the trauma of the operation caused this retrograde amnesia, which in the course of time became less severe, that is, events preceding the operation were better remembered.

As more rigorously tested by events and features, HM has been found to have a retrograde amnesia for one to three years before the hippocampectomy. Larry Squire finds a similar duration of retrograde amnesia after bilateral electroshock therapy. The period of sensitivity to disruption correlates with observations on the normal course of forgetting. Thus there would seem to be a period of one to three years involved in the process of consolidation of a long-term memory so that it is no longer susceptible to loss in the process of forgetting or in the process of memory disruption by bilateral hippocampectomy or electroshock therapy. We have now to envisage that in order to effect a "permanent" consolidation of a memory, the hippocampal input to the neocortex must be replayed much as in the initial experience in what we may name "recall episodes" for one to three years. Failure of this replay results in the ordinary process of forgetting. After three years the memory codes in the patterns of potentiated synapses in the cerebral cortex are much more securely established and apparently require no further adjuventating hippocampal inputs; hence they are not lost in the disruption of bilateral hippocampectomy or electroconvulsive therapy.

Conclusions

The ability to learn came very early in the evolution of the nervous system. Remarkable studies on the learning processes of invertebrates and of lower vertebrates have been made. Modifiable synapses have been identified in many nervous sytems. As already mentioned, motor learning involves quite different parts of the brain. Our concern in this chapter has been to trace the evolutionary process at its pinnacle of achievement in the human brain. And cognitive memory must rank at the summit of the human memory processes, because it concerns the storage and retrieval of conscious experiences.

Of course much of our memory is implicit, giving each of us our character in its widest sense. It is involved in our personal formation from the earliest childhood learning of the mother tongue, for example, right up to the present time. As a consequence we come to look at things differently and to react differently, but this is not consciously recognized by us, or only very dimly. It is implicit in our whole cultural formation, as in Figure 3–4.

This chapter has dealt with the much more recognizable *explicit memory*. In this memory *Homo sapiens* is supreme. The range of memory is unbelievably large. We have immense "data banks" with literally millions of stored memories. The difficulty is in retrieval, which becomes progressively more difficult with age, in part at least because of the progressively increasing storage.

We postulate that there is another memory. It is in World 2, not in the brain, as is shown in the box to the right of Figure 3–1. In the first place it functions in the attempt to recall a memory. This must be an active selection process exerted on cortical modules. In the second place it has a recognition role, judging the correctness of the retrieved memory, as experienced consciously, e.g. of a name or a number. If the readout from the data banks is judged as faulty, then it can reinstitute the search.

The cerebral mechanisms here postulated for cognitive memory must be regarded as an attempt to build up an explanatory hypothesis that is in accord with present knowledge and that challenges experimental testing.

Undoubtedly the hypotheses developed for brain–mind interaction in memory storage and retrieval are still provisional. In particular the brain–mind problem is central to the problem of cognitive memory. What is utterly mysterious is that the human brain was evolved for survival in a primitive community, yet it came to have immense and wonderful performances in cognitive memory. Contrast the poverty of the chimpanzee's abilities with the richness of the human performance. A concluding remark: In reading this memory chapter your own personal experiences should be kept in mind. We thus come to two cryptic summarizing statements on cognitive memory: Without memory no consciousness; without consciousness no memory.

It is clear from what we have said about learning and memory that simple schemes to account for them are incompatible with the facts as these have emerged from studies of brain mechanisms and from reflections on our own experiences. Yet the complexities of learning and memory seem to be diminished when we confront the broader and richer domain of human *intelligence* as we attempt to show in the next chapter.

Suggested Readings

ECCLES, J. C. *Facing reality.* Heidelberg: Springer Verlag, 1970, Ch. 3.

ECCLES, J. C. *The understanding of the brain.* New York: McGraw-Hill, 1973, Ch. 5.

ECCLES, J. C. *The human mystery.* Berlin, Heidelberg, New York: Springer Verlag Internat., 1979, Ch. 9.

ECCLES, J. C. *The human psyche.* Berlin, Heidelberg, New York: Springer Verlag Internat., 1980, Ch. 7.

MILNER, B. Amnesia following operation on the temporal lobes. In C. W. M. Whitty and O. L. Zangwill (Eds.), *Amensia.* London: Butterworths, 1966.

PENFIELD, W. *The mystery of the mind.* Princeton, N.J.: Princeton University Press, 1975.

POPPER, K. R. and ECCLES, J. C. *The self and its brain.* Berlin, Heidelberg, New York: Springer Verlag Internat., 1977, Chs. P2, P4, E8, Dialogues VI, VII.

VICTOR, M., ADAMS, R. D., and COLLINS, G. H. *The Wernicke-Korsakoff-Syndrome.* Oxford: Blackwell Scientific, 1971, pp. 1–206.

10

Intelligence—
Artificial and Real

Intelligence, Evolution,
and the Hypothesis of Uniformity

It is common for contemporary defenders of Darwinism to insist that human psychological attributes can only be modifications and quantitative extensions of characteristics found among all primates and even all mammals. But this argument is based on a less than acute comprehension of the principles of modern evolutionary theory and genetics. Indeed, if we take the defenders of Darwinism as upholding a *uniformity* thesis according to which the fundamental psychological equipment of the animal kingdom is uniformly distributed within the kingdom, then we must conclude that such defenders are actually at odds with the facts and principles of genetic science.

The uniformity thesis is generally upheld by today's radical environmentalists, especially those who call themselves "behavioral scientists." They seem to think it is by way of this thesis that their own specialty takes on respectable (Darwinian) scientific credentials. They confuse the uniform *operation* of natural selection with a uniform *consequence* of natural selection. Modern evolutionary theory subscribes, as Darwin did, to the former but specifically rejects the latter. What the demands of the environment are "selecting" ultimately is a given *genotype,* a given constellation of genes leading to the survival of the organism whose phenotypic characteristics have been built by the coded information in the genotype (Figure 6–1). As the environment undergoes alterations, some of them sudden and ruthless, the affected organisms must adapt or perish. There are two chief modes of adaptation. For the species as a whole, survival depends upon the existence of members able to meet the challenge by virtue of possessing a genetic constitution that allows a sufficiently wide physiological *reaction range.* Thus, some members of the species will be able to survive at uncommonly cold temperatures or with extremely reduced consumption of food or water or after the appearance of a particularly adept predator. The genetic combinations carried by successful members of the species now have, in such conditions, a greater probability of surviving (in the offspring generations) than have those combinations carried by unsuccessful members. Over the long haul, then, certain genes occur more frequently and others less frequently in the overall *gene pool* of the species. This is the process that has been richly exploited in animal husbandry and agronomy since remote antiquity.

The second mode of adaptation is genetic *mutation,* by which an entirely new genotype appears within the species. Such mutations can be produced chemically or, today, by using carrier viruses, which invade the cells of the host animal. In nature, however, the vast majority of mutant genes turn out to have lethal and monstrous consequences. On those occasions when mutations lead to especially adaptive effects, however, the mutant species survives and gives rise to a new species, which could not have arisen from the genetic combinations existing in the gene pool of the established species.

It is well known in animal husbandry that desirable traits can be successively refined and made "true" by inbreeding. The characteristics (*phenotypes*) chosen are those that appear throughout the species but not as frequently or to the desired degree. By mating those possessing the phenotypes to an unusual degree, it is possible to concentrate the responsible genes in the offspring generation. And by inbreeding the offspring, still another generation is produced in which the "selected" genotype is even purer for the traits in question. In such cases the phenotypes are said to result from additive genetic factors in that each of the individual genes makes some contribution to the desired traits. It is through this selective manipulation of gene frequencies within a species that different *varieties* occur either naturally or by intentional breeding. Thus we produce not new species but new varieties. In such contexts it makes sense to speak of the traits in question as falling along a quantitative continuum of, for example, color, height, weight, speed, or endurance. To put the matter simply, we may say of such traits that they are uniformly present in the species but occur only very rarely in the degree displayed by the selectively bred sample, that is, by this new (or emerging) variety.

In comparing entirely different species, however, we are dealing not with additive genetic factors but with entirely different genotypes. What we have is not "more of the same" phenotypes but utterly unique ones. The bird's wing is not "more of a fin" or a "better fin"; it is not a fin at all. Again, the fallacy of origins (FOO) noted in earlier chapters encourages some to think that the essential nature of a given species is unearthed when we dig deeply enough into its phylogenetic past. The same counterfeit Darwinist who thinks of man as an especially clever ape is required by the logic of his "science" to think of birds as especially agile fish! It is then a relatively small step to conclude that the ape taught a sign language is providing proof that human language is not "special" or "unique."

The plain fact is that every species is unique and special which, after all, is what we mean by *species* in the first place. Because of this, there is surely no scientific reason to expect that different species will adapt in a uniform way to the demands of the environment. Two different species placed in the *physically* same environment are, in fact, in radically different *biological* environments calling forth appropriately different modes of adaptation. If natural selection operates uniformly on all species, its consequences *must* differ from species to species. Accordingly, if one subscribes in the most orthodox way to the teachings of neo-Darwinian biology and modern genetics, one has no reason at all to expect adaptive uniformities across species. No one, that is, has any reason to expect that a man will be any more "like" an ape than a fish is "like" a duck. Since different species are involved, the kinship of the most remote (and allegedly common) ancestors is quite beside the point. The occurrence of those mutations that gave both ape and man the *qualitatively* different and new genotypes they now possess made both unlike the remote "parent" stock and unlike each other.

How unlike? This, as it happens, is an empirical question to be addressed in the laboratory and in the natural habitats of both species. It is not to be answered by a "theory" or by those uncritical metaphors that now pass for evolutionary science. As is to be expected, our answers to the "How unlike?" question will depend upon the specific phenotypes chosen for comparison. Ape and man both have two legs—though discriminably different even as legs go!—but so do birds. Apes solve problems quickly, but so do the rat, the racoon, and the gerbil. That the ape can more quickly solve problems than other animals—except the human animal—may suggest no more than that apes and human beings were groomed under more similar selection pressures. Nonetheless, apes do not write cantatas and do not trouble themselves with metaphysics. They are apes, a good thing to be for an ape. The "How unlike?" question must pertain to *qualitative* features, which are extremely difficult to define. As our subject is *personhood,* the ones that come most readily to mind are the features of intellect and morals. Having treated of the latter, we shall examine intellect in this chapter, recognizing it to be unmatched and, in revealing ways, unheralded in the animal kingdom. By now it should be clear, however, that this fact need not embarrass the informed evolutionist and geneticist, but only the fashionable polemicist who attracts a crowd with empty generalization.

Intelligence and Learning

Contemporary psychologists remain in healthy disagreement over the issue of intelligence, especially the proper means of its assessment. The "IQ" test pleases almost no one who has given sustained attention to the matter, even though the measures yielded by such tests do predict academic and certain career performances.

The critics of IQ testing have always been numerous. In recent decades they have also been vociferous, in part because of their not too veiled radical-environmentalist metaphysics and in part because of the sloppy hereditarianism that some have found defended by the IQ testing of various racial groups. Courts in California have ruled against the use of such tests in assigning children to such special categories as *Educable–Mentally Retarded* (E–M), grounding their rulings in the fact that children of African and Hispanic origins are "disproportionately" found in the E–M category. Here we have evidence of environmentalism run amok. Jurists apparently have decided that *all* human phenotypes must be "proportionately" represented among the various ethnic and racial groups comprised by the human community. To reach their decisions the judges must conclude that the scores attained by children are reflections of environmental conditions. But in this the judges surely must accept that *something* is being measured, if only the quality of local schools and home life. If this is so, then the tests serve the worthwhile function of "calibrating" the quality of nurturing environments and should therefore be *compulsory*! How else can citizens determine if their children are receiving a just share of educational resources?

Others have found in the results additional evidence to support the thesis that certain "groups" are simply not very intelligent. Here we have hereditarianism run amok. Caucasian children from caring homes also fall into the E–M category, and both Afro-American and Hispano-American children can attain exceptionally high scores. Any simple "racial" explanation of the findings is bankrupt of logic. We inherit our parents' genes, not their traits. There is no "IQ gene." Genes are complex molecules; nucleotide sequences of DNA carrying the code for building specific proteins. The DNA carries many tens of thousands of such genes, which build enzymes and other proteins able to regulate the metabolic physiology of the cells of the body and thereby control the functions by which essential proteins, enzymes, hormones, and other cellular products are formed. In cases of severe (pathological) deficiencies, profound mental impoverishment may ensue. (In the California sample, the incidence of gene-based mental retardation was the same among Afro-American, Hispano-American, and "white" children.) Outcomes of this sort are almost invariably associated with the actual absence or with the mutation of genes, and the mental consequences are but part of a generally pathological picture. Where a child is *educable,* however, the genetic explanation of retardation is most suspect. Indeed, any explanation based on the notion of an "intelligence gene" must be suspect, for it involves a conflation of radically different processes: the purely biological processes of growth and physiological health and the neurological and psychological processes that include (but are not limited to) learning, memory, attention, motivation, emotion— *human character* and its ineffables. The way to test hereditarianism, of course, is to give every child the opportunities and encouragements known to nurture the lively mind and to see how far that child can progress under such conditions. To dismiss the child's potential for achievement on the basis of an examination or, worse, because the child is the member of some race or group is nothing less than sinful. And for a court to rule against the very tests that permit us to assess the particular needs and deficits of each child—and to do so in the name of some nonsensical egalitarian philosophy—is nothing less than judicial malfeasance. It would be a sin for the judge who knew better.

For a child to be tested it must know something, if only the meaning of ''Please sit down.'' Some have argued, therefore, that so-called intelligence tests can be tests only of what children have already learned, not of their ''potential.'' Of course, what one has already learned is at least a rough measure of ''potential,'' but it is also a rough measure of *opportunities for learning.* Some leaders in the field of mental testing have attempted to distinguish between two kinds of intelligence—''fluid'' and ''crystallized''—only one of which directly affects ''potential.'' By *crystallized* intelligence psychologists refer to those mental tasks that can be completed only after certain fundamental abilities have been learned. We all know of children who are very good at arithmetic and algebra or who have well-developed vocabularies or who follow instructions to the letter. Such children often attain outstanding academic records and, as the expression goes, are never heard from again. We need consider only the professional mnemonist whose feats of memory are nearly incredible, or those eidetic children with so-called *photographic memories,* able to recite whole pages of text after but a moment's examination. In these instances we have evidence of a kind of intelligence, but surely not the kind we ordinarily ascribe to a Newton, Galileo, or Einstein.

Fluid intelligence, on the other hand, refers to one's ability to find the solution to entirely new problems where prior learning is largely irrelevant. The words ''insight'' and ''imagination'' are often used to characterize the mental ability of those who excel at such undertakings. Their intellectual achievements may emerge from modest or even inadequate learning.

Modern psychology has only just begun to respect the great variety of cognitive types and styles displayed by different persons and by the same person from childhood to maturity. There is still no adequate theory to account for the genius. Neither radical hereditarianism nor radical environmentalism can stand up to the facts about such persons. Their pedigrees, their early environments, their formal schooling, and their personalities provide no firm or reliable commonalities. What is clear is that intellect alone is not enough to explain a Shakespeare, Beethoven, or Newton. Intertwined with the accomplishments of such persons are the complexities of motivation, conviction, and a transcendent inspiration that somehow elevates the *psyche* above the commoner habits of mind and feeling. Learning and memory have, it would seem, very little to do with creativity at this level, and by implication we might conclude further that learning and memory have little to do with creativity at even lower levels of human enterprise.

There is, then, this enlarged sense of *intelligence* not embraced by the facts and theories pertaining to learning, instinct, or memory and therefore not illuminated by comparative studies of the performances of lower organisms. Darwin was led astray by his anthropomorphic penchants. He concluded that the human mind falls on that *continuum of mind* occupied by all of the advanced species, but he arrived at this conclusion chiefly by overestimating the cognitive element in the activities of nonhuman animals. And, of course, he did this for the quite understandable reason that he assumed his evolutionary theory was as applicable to human psychology as it was to phylogenetic diversity. As with his less famous contemporaries, Darwin too spoke innocently of the ant's "armies," complete with field commanders and infantry; of the sexual "enticement" achieved by the male bird through his colorful plumage. Darwin reckoned that the uniform operation of natural selection favored the proliferation of certain habitual (instinctive) modes of adaptation. Since craft and cunning were essential to all of the advanced species, the human mind could be no more than an evolved apparatus able to do much better the sorts of things done by the minds of animals. As William James would observe,

> So it has come to pass that the instincts of animals are ransacked to throw light on our own; and that the reasoning faculties of bees and ants, the minds of savages and infants, madmen, idiots, the deaf and the blind, criminals, and eccentrics, are all invoked in support of this or that special theory. . . . The interpretation of the "psychoses" of animals, savages, and infants is necessarily wild work, in which the personal equation of the investigator has things very much its own way. [*Principles of Psychology,* Vol. 1, p. 194]

After a century of such efforts it should be possible to praise Darwin but to bury this theoretical dead end of vintage Darwinism. The productions of human intelligence are *sui generis* and are anticipated nowhere in (mere) nature. To attempt to explain this intelligence by "ransacking" the instincts of animals or timing them in mazes or counting the pellets of food they obtain by pressing on a bar is finally "wild work." There is some scientific merit in examining the behavior of lower organisms when that behavior closely matches human behavior under the same or highly similar conditions. Such research is as potentially useful as are studies of digestion or reproduction or respiration in different species. The danger, however, is that the investigator who discovers *some* common features across species will conclude that there is *nothing* different about them. Psychology has victimized itself in this regard by choosing tasks that animals can perform and then having human beings engage in the same tasks. Naturally, all we will learn from such research is that man is "like" any number of animals in *some* respects. But man is utterly unlike *any* animal in other respects, and this is a fact that will not go away. It is the uniqueness of the human person that must be the starting point of any mature psychology, should such a discipline ever come into being.

Artificial Intelligence

The appearance of high-speed digital computers helped to revive the mechanistic psychology of the eighteenth century, when some of the better minds insisted that man was no more than "an enlightened machine." Advances in programming and in circuit design have now led to electronic devices that perform a wide variety of functions more quickly and with far greater accuracy than mere mortals can claim. And so we have become accustomed to such claims as "Computers think," and "The mind is just a computer, and not a very good one."

Philosophers, too, have entered the debate and have argued carefully for a theory of mind grounded in the principles of computer science. In this they have been joined by leading scientists in cognitive psychology as well as by logicians, mathematicians, and engineers. An entire subspecialty has formed, artificial intelligence (AI), devoted to the study of machine simulations of human problem-solving and cognition. It would seem that the AI community divides itself into those who would look to computers to do the sorts of things we do not do well and those who would equate everything we do mentally with functions also performed by machines. It is this latter perspective that warrants comment here.

The argument for the human mind as a computer takes this general form: (1) All experience and thought are made possible by the brain; (2) the brain itself is an elaborate computer, its synaptic junctions having "on–off" functions and its nerves having signal-processing functions; (3) as modern computer science has shown (and as the mathematical logician A. M. Turing argued nearly a half-century ago), all decision functions are reducible to a binary yes–no process; (4) there is nothing in *experience* other than a form of symbolic coding and nothing in *mentation* other than various binary modes of decision-making. A developed cognitive science, then, is one that has learned how the brain's symbols represent the external world and how the brain's circuitry regulates the processing of "input."

This has now been said a thousand times, in books and journals and from the lectern, so that nontechnical audiences have come to accept their pitiful ignorance as the reason for their incredulity. But hidden in this breathless litany of declarations and "therefores" is a conceptual dilemma of the first order. Let us begin to recognize this dilemma by noting that we do not "experience" our own discharging neurons, we experience what is *in the world*. When we look at a landscape, for example, we do not see so many neural impulses, we see trees and mountains and the horizon. Experience, therefore, has a *psychological* property not possessed by any physiological event or process.

This brings us directly to the alleged "symbols" in the brain, the "codes" by which neural or neurochemical events come to *stand for* various psychological attributes. According to this hypothesis, the external world impinges on our sense organs, which convert ("code") the incoming signals neurophysiologically. The brain then processes these codes and, through some sort of *translation algorithm,* converts the processed neurophysiological data into that "psychological" format with which consciousness is filled.

This line of explanation comes directly from computer science. When the keyboard of the computer terminal is used, the letters and numbers typed lead to electrical pulses in the computer's "hardware." Thus, we are able to go from the level of letter symbols to the level of electronic signals, the latter serving as a coded form of the former. Within the computer's circuits these signals are processed, and then, through a set of preprogrammed commands or rules (that is, through the appropriate *algorithm*) the processed electrical signals are reported out in the form of an intelligible series of words and numbers.

That there are parallels between the computer's performance and human cognition becomes less surprising once we realize that it is human cognition that has programmed the computer and that makes "symbols" possible in the first place. Note that the computer's hardware is always and only generating electrical pulses. *We* are the ones who wire the device in such a way that a series of pulses will illuminate a screen with ''Flight 202 has been delayed.'' The computer no more knows that a flight has been delayed than a tape recorder knows how to sing *La Traviata*. But beyond this all too obvious fact is the curious notion of a *translation algorithm* ascribed to the human brain. We can design computer circuits and program computers in such a way that a given series of pulses *stands for,* for example, ''Flight 202.'' Morse Code does just this sort of ''translating'' of dots and dashes into words and sentences. But what does it mean to say that the *brain* engages in translations of this sort, and what does it mean to say that it achieves these translations by way of a set of rules or algorithms? The reason we can go from Morse Code to a grammatical and informative sentence is that we have adopted the convention of treating patterns of dots and dashes as words and punctuation marks. That is, having full knowledge of *both* Morse Code *and* English words thus coded, we can move from one format to the other. What is true here is true of every translation from one language to another; *viz.,* a knowledge of *both* languages. Indeed, the very concept of translation *entails* a knowledge of *other languages*.

But this is just where the AI theory of human cognition breaks down. For the brain to possess the *translation algorithm* needed to convert neurophysiological ''symbols'' into a format having psychological attributes, the brain would have to have knowledge of *both* languages, which is to say it would have to know its own language and—who else's? Are there really *two* entities engaged in this translation, the brain and the person whose brain it is? Even this odd arrangement would do no good, however, for the brain would still have to know both its own internal language and the language of the experiencer.

If, on the other hand, there is only the brain—and not some superadded ''person''—then we have the strange case of our (the brain's) having to learn our (its) own language, for this after all is what must be meant when we are told that the chief task of the neural sciences is to ''learn the language of the brain.'' The plain fact is that unless we (our brains) are in possession of *both* languages, no translation from a physiological to a psychological format is possible. And if we (our brains) are in possession of *both* languages, it is surprising that after three hundred years of tireless research we are still so ignorant of one of them.

The search for ''symbols'' in the brain must be aimless, for there are no symbols in the brain, only in the remarks we make about the brain. There are, alas, no symbols in computers either, only pulses and pauses. The brain is, indeed, an extraordinary computer whose workings are fantastic. The serious scientist has every reason to study these workings and to help us understand how this unique device serves us throughout life. That it does have its own "language" is evidence enough of a division between the computer and the programmer, between it and its owner. But brain, *qua* brain, cannot be the "I" in reports of experience and of thought. In an ironic way, the brain does possess an *artificial intelligence* in that it does its necessary work oblivious to the mission it serves, the mission of personhood.

Suggested Readings

DRETSKE, F. *Knowledge and the flow of information.* Oxford: Basil Blackwell, 1981.

GUILFORD, J. P. *The nature of human intelligence.* New York: McGraw-Hill, 1967.

NEWELL, A., and SIMON, H. *Human problem solving.* Englewood Cliffs, N. J.: Prentice-Hall, 1972.

RAPHAEL, B. *The thinking computer.* San Francisco: W. H. Freeman, 1976.

11

Voluntary Movement, Freedom of the Will, Moral Responsibility

We have the indubitable experience that by thinking and willing we can control our actions if we so wish, such actions being called *voluntary movements*. The sequence can be expressed as motive (thinking) → intention (willing) → voluntary action. In bringing about movement voluntarily some brain events are initiated. There is the well-known crossed pyramidal tract from the *motor cortex* down the spinal cord to the nerve cells of the opposite side that cause the muscles to contract. The motor cortex is a narrow band of the cerebral cortex running over its convexity from the midline near the vertex. This is shown for the left hemisphere in Figure 11-1. The various parts of the limbs, face, and body are represented in a striplike map. This map is constructed from the movements that result from electrical stimulation at sites along the strip, e.g. when the region marked "thumb" is stimulated, the thumb on the opposite side moves. In this way it is shown

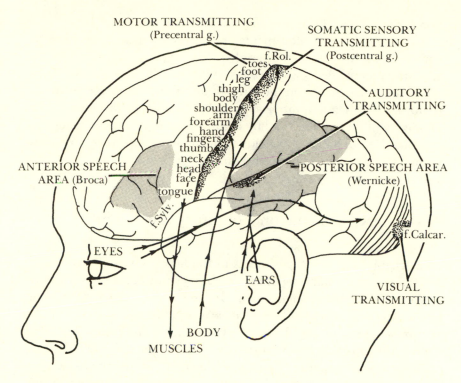

FIGURE 11-1. The Motor and Sensory Transmitting Areas of the Cerebral Cortex. The approximate map of the motor transmitting areas is shown in the precentral gyrus, while the somatic sensory receiving areas are in a similar map in the postcentral gyrus. Actually the toes, foot, and leg should be represented over the top on the medial surface. Other primary sensory areas shown are the visual and auditory, but they are largely in areas screened from this lateral view. Also shown are the speech areas of Broca and Wernicke. Arrows show inputs from eyes, ears, and body (tactile) going to the respective primary cortical areas. From motor transmitting area arrows show projection downward to muscles.

that the left motor cortex of Figure 11-1 controls the right side of the body and vice versa. It might be thought that voluntary movement is so explained, but the reality is enormously more complicated and only partly understood. The pyramidal cells of the motor cortex discharge impulses down the pyramidal tract to motoneurons in the spinal cord that control movement. But this is only the last stage of the brain events concerned in voluntary movement. There are two fundamental problems: (1) In the initiation of a voluntary movement by a *motive → intention,* what are the sequences of events being set up in the brain? Moreover, (2) what brain machinery is brought into action to ensure that the desired movements are carried out? It has to be recognized that some movements are simply too fast for there to be control by feedback from the periphery, e.g. typing, playing a percussion instrument, fast speaking, fast writing. These fast movements are entirely dependent on the burst of impulses discharged from the motor cortex, being appropriately called "ballistic" because of the analogy with the bullets fired by a gun. Most of our movements are combinations of ballistic and slower movements (called ramp movements) that are subject to control during performance, just as occurs with a target-finding missile.

Experiments on Voluntary Movement

Remarkable series of experiments in the last few years have transformed our understanding of the cerebral events concerned with the initiation of a voluntary movement. It can now be stated that the first brain reactions caused by the *intention to move* are in nerve cells of the *supplementary motor area* (*SMA*), which is indicated in Figure 8–2. It is right at the top of the brain, mostly on the medial surface as is shown. This area was recognized by the renowned neurosurgeon Wilder Penfield when he was stimulating the exposed human brain in the search for epileptic "foci" (regions of aberrant activity associated with epileptic seizures). Stimulation of this area did not cause the sharply localized responses indicated in Figure 11–1 for the motor cortex. Instead there were writhing or adversive movements of large parts of the torso and limbs, even of the same side, and also incoherent vocalizations. So this area was neglected for decades, as it did not seem to have an interesting function. Now, from this Cinderella status, the SMA has been advanced to a role of highest interest because of the experimental evidence from three laboratories.

First is the research of Robert Porter and Cobie Brinkman. In their studies a monkey has recording microelectrodes surgically implanted in the SMA. After recovery, the monkey initiates voluntary movements by pulling a lever in a self-paced manner with either hand in order to obtain a food-reward. It is found that with this voluntary act many of the nerve cells of the SMA begin to discharge well before the cells in the motor cortex and indeed before any other nerve cells of the brain, except for a small focus in the premotor cortex, which is just anterior to the motor cortex, indicated by PM in Figure 8–2.

Since the complex movement is caused by many muscles contracting in sequence, it can be anticipated that only some of the SMA nerve cells would be concerned in the muscle contraction initiating the lever-pulling. But it is impressive that many of the sample of several hundred SMA nerve cells were firing probably about one-tenth of a second *before* the earliest discharge of the pyramidal cells down to the spinal cord. An important finding is that the nerve cells of one SMA are activated whether the monkey chooses to use the right or the left hand in the lever-pull, with more activity as a rule associated with a contralateral pull. This may relate to the crossed activity of the motor cortex.

Second is the research of Nils Lassen, Per Roland, and their group in Copenhagen. For more than a decade advantage has been taken of the insertion of a canula into the internal carotid artery of patients in order to study the cerebral circulation (*angiography*).

In a radiotracer technique, radio-xenon is injected through this canula into the cerebral circulation, and, with a battery of 254 radiation detectors assembled in a helmet over the scalp, the circulation of blood can be simultaneously measured from that number of areas in a mosaic map of the cerebral cortex. The activity of nerve cells is accurately signaled by an increase in the circulation of blood. In this way, during the carrying out of a wide variety of actions, the activities of the nerve cells of the cerebral cortex are measured and, by an exquisite technique, are immediately converted into a map of the cerebral cortex, color-coded for percentages of activity falling above or below the resting background. It is a wonderful technique and gives most impressive results, but there are two disabilities. First, it takes about forty seconds of exposure to secure one picture. Second, the grain of the picture mosaic is rather coarse, the units of the mosaic being about one square centimeter or one-sixth of a square inch.

In this research a voluntary movement is chosen so that the patient has to concentrate continuously. The task is practiced by the patient before the test so that it is well carried out. In a particularly significant test—called the motor sequence test—the thumb has to touch in quick succession finger 1 twice, finger 2 once, finger 3 three times, finger 4 twice. A new sequence with minimal pause begins with finger 4 touched twice, the patient now performing the original sequence in reverse order; then in the initial order; then in reverse order, and so forth throughout the test. These movements require continuous voluntary attention and never become automatic. The invariable finding is that there are highly significant increases (about 30 percent) in blood flow in the hand area of the contralateral motor cortex (Figure 11–2A) and in the adjacent sensory area, as would be expected, and also in the SMAs (almost 30 percent) of both hemispheres. There could, of course, be no evidence as to the priority of the SMA activation. This evidence was, however, obtained by a remarkable variant of the experiment that is called *internal programming*. The subject had to carry out the same motor sequence test but *mentally* without any movement whatsoever. This motor silence was checked by electromyography, a technique whereby even extremely subtle muscular contractions can be detected. As would be expected, there was no trace of activity in the motor cortex or the adjacent sensory cortex, but, wonderful to relate (Figure 11–2B), the SMAs of both sides were activated almost as much as for the movement sequences, whereas all other brain areas showed no significant increase in activity. So it can be concluded that, in the intending of a movement, nerve cells in the SMA are the first to be called into action. In the so-called *internal programming,* the mental intention initiates in the SMA, and nowhere else, the activity appropriate for the voluntary movement. Yet at the same time the mental influence restrains this activity from spreading elsewhere through the brain and so causing the motor cortex discharge down the spinal cord with the ensuing voluntary movement.

This finding closely parallels that of the first research program (Porter and Brinkman) on the nerve cells of the monkey's SMA, which in a voluntary movement often fired well before the cells of the motor cortex and other areas of the brain. A complementary finding in the radio-xenon experiments was that, with such simple movements as finger-wagging or continuous pressure on a spring by thumb and forefinger, no activity of the SMA accompanied the activity of the motor cortex and its associated sensory cortex. Doubtless a brief initial activity of the SMA was required to initiate the movement, but thereafter voluntary intention gave place to automatism. During the continuous voluntary intention required for the motor sequence test it is impossible to carry out a meaningful and subtle conversation. In contrast this can be done during continuous finger-wagging or the exertion of pressure once such action has become automatic. These radio-xenon tests for SMA activity thus distinguish between voluntary and automatic movements.

Third is the research of Hans Kornhüber and Luder Deecke, who in the 1960s described the activity of the cerebral cortex before

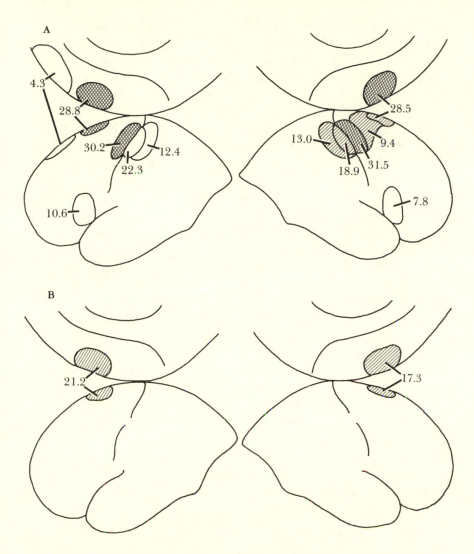

FIGURE 11-2. A Mean Increase of the rCBF in Percentage During the Motor-sequence Test Performed by the Contralateral Hand. Corrected for diffuse increase of the blood flow. Cross-hatched areas have an increase of rCBF significant at the 0.0005 level. Hatched areas have an increase of rCBF significant at the 0.005 level; for other areas shown the rCBF increase is significant at the level 0.05. Left: left hemisphere, five subjects. Right: right hemisphere, ten subjects. B. Mean Increase of rCBF in Percentage During Internal Programming of the Motor-sequence Test. Values corrected for diffuse increase of the blood flow. Left: left hemisphere, three subjects; right: right hemisphere, five subjects. [Figure from P. E. Roland, B. Larsen, N. A. Lassen, and E. Skinhøj, *J. Neurophysiol.* 43 (1980): 118–36]

the carrying out of a voluntary act. By an ingenious storage and averaging technique, the minute brain potentials* recorded from the scalp were studied. Almost one second before carrying out a simple voluntary movement such as bending a finger, the patient's brain displays a gradually increasing negative electrical potential. This is called the *readiness potential* and is found to be greatest in amplitude over the SMA, though it is also large over the motor cortex and the adjacent (premotor and parietal) areas. It tends to become especially large over the area of the motor cortex involved in the movement. However, its distribution lacks any sharp focusing that could give evidence as to the site of action of the mental intention. It was generally regarded as showing that, in initiating a voluntary movement, the mental act of intention was exerted on widely dispersed areas of the cerebral cortex. More recently, however, studies on the readiness potential of patients with bilateral Parkinsonism have revealed that it is initiated in the region of the SMA. These patients suffer from a great difficulty in initiating voluntary movement (*akinesia*). Correspondingly the readiness potential over the motor cortex is greatly depressed. Nevertheless, the readiness potential is fully developed over the SMA. Evidently the patient has no disability with respect to the act of intention initiating a full response of the SMA. The disability must instead be in the pathway from the SMA to the motor cortex. This inference is in accord with the evidence that the Parkinsonian akinesia is due to damage to the pathway from the premotor area of the cortex—including the SMA—to the basal ganglia and so to the motor cortex, a loop that provides what is called *striato-fugal drive* to the motor cortex. It can be concluded that this evidence again demonstrates the priority of the SMA in the initiation of a voluntary act.

Mental Intentions and Movement

Thus there is strong support for the hypothesis that the SMA is the sole recipient area of the brain for mental intentions that lead to voluntary movements. This is a most important improvement on the concept that the mental act of intention to move was widely dispersed in its action on the brain. Such a sharp focusing lends precision to our attempts to define the manner in which some particular voluntary action is brought about. The concept of motor programs is important in

*Electrical signals which, at the surface of the scalp, are measured in millionths of a volt but can be summed for repeated activities.

this enterprise. Instead of just waving our arms or indulging in some other crude movement to display intention leading to action, we have to recognize the complexity of the muscle actions in bringing about any skilled and learned movement. It can be as commonplace as extending one's hand to pick up a cup and, in an elegant and smooth action, to bring the cup to one's lips for a drink, thereafter placing the cup back in its saucer. A most complex series of movements has been accomplished, each movement of which can be reduced to some constituent motor programs; putting one's hand to the cup; securely grasping the handle; smoothly lifting the cup; bringing it correctly to the lips; drinking, which is a whole series of lip, tongue, pharyngeal, and swallowing movements; and finally the return of the cup. Thus there is a whole interlocking series of movements involving contraction of a large number of muscles, all nicely graded and sequenced. It is convenient to describe this complex movement as being composed of a harmony of elemental motor programs.

Let us now consider how our intention to enact such a voluntary movement can be related to the role of the SMA as the mediator between the mental act of intention and the assemblage of motor programs involved in the voluntary movement. We must first postulate that the mental intention acts on the SMA in a highly selective way, and that the SMA contains, as it were, an inventory of all the learned motor programs. This immense stored repertoire of the learned motor programs of a lifetime could not be stored in the SMA, which is a quite limited area of the cerebral cortex with perhaps 50 million neurons and 15,000 modules on each side. All that is necessary is for the SMA to contain *the inventory of the motor programs*, which comprises addresses to the storage banks of the motor programs. The SMA is known to have major lines of communication to the presumed storage sites in the cerebral cortex (particularly the premotor cortex, PM in Figure 8–2) and in the basal ganglia and the cerebellum. By the radiotracer techniques these areas have been shown to be called into action in voluntary movements, and many nerve cells in these circuits have been shown to be active probably before the discharge of the motor cortical cells.

Thus we have in outline a hypothesis of how the mental act of intention can, by action through the SMA, bring about the desired movement. There is an immense literature on this subject as well as on the disorders of movements resulting from clinical lesions of the components of the circuits. It may seem that an extraordinary complexity of neural machinery has been introduced to account for the carrying out of a simple act such as raising a cup to the lips—which we accomplish without reflection. But any obscurantist temptations would be resisted if something went wrong with the neural machinery of the subject who, for example, might well be a philosopher who hitherto had recognized no mysterious happenings between intention and action!

Let us now return to the performance of the nerve cells of the SMA when the monkey is pulling the lever in a voluntary act. A single nerve cell under observation will be firing at the usual slow and irregular frequency, the background discharge. Then there is a sharp increase of the frequency of firing and in a little more than a fifth of a second the movement starts. We could in fact predict the onset of the movement from the observed discharges of the nerve cell. It is important to recognize that this burst of discharge of the observed SMA cell was not triggered by some other nerve cell of the SMA or elsewhere in the brain. The first discharges occur in the SMA, as is also shown in the radio-xenon studies of internal programming. So we have here an irrefutable demonstration that a mental act of intention *initiates* the burst of discharges of a nerve cell. Furthermore, when hundreds of SMA nerve cells are observed, only some are activated at this early stage. Others come later, others may fire in two successive bursts, and still others are even silenced. And these specific types of response are repeatedly displayed by any nerve cell in relation to a particular voluntary act. Thus we have to postulate that the mental act of intention was being effective in a discriminating fashion. There was observed in fact a most complex pattern of neuronal responses of the SMA nerve cells. So the mental act of intention is exerted in a subtle discriminating fashion on the constituent nerve cells of the SMAs on each side.

A particular intention—in this case the monkey's intention to pull the lever—is conveyed in the form of a discriminating code to the SMA neurons. This code must have a spatiotemporal pattern, for the action proceeds in space and time. We have entered into a field of discourse where discriminating mental events have highly selective actions on the SMA neurons. Presumably the mental influences are exerted by a code in a graded and varied manner and are subject to feedback influences from the activated SMA neurons. The frontier between mental events and neural events must be traversable in both directions (cf. Figure 3–1). It is evident that we have embarked upon a temerarious field of speculation. But the facts remain that we can carry out skilled and learned movements "at will"; that immensely complicated neural machinery is necessary for any such act; and that the mental influences must work in a coded manner on the SMA neurons and generate corresponding codes of spatiotemporal patterns in the discharges of the SMA neurons. Each such pattern presumably is an inventory of motor programs with the addresses for transmitting the codes so as to institute the activities of these motor programs.

Several questions can be raised. (1) How can the mental act of intention activate across the mind–brain frontier those particular SMA neurons in the appropriate code for instituting the motor programs that bring about intended voluntary movements? The general answer is that this is the learned procedure of a lifetime, from babyhood onward, but of course there is as yet little understanding of how that learning can come about. (2) How does the proposed interaction of mind and brain relate to the "free will" problem? The answer is that, despite the so-called insuperable difficulty of having a nonmaterial mind act on a material brain, it has been demonstrated to occur by a mental intention in just the manner predicted by dualist-interactionism—no doubt to the great discomfiture of all materialists and physicalists. Their own critical assessments of the research will be most revealing. (3) To what extent is the *liaison brain* (Figure 3–1) for intention the liaison brain for other mental acts? For the mental process of silent counting the liaison area is found by Lassen to be just anterior to the SMA. Silent counting is a purely cognitive act and does not involve the intention to act, as is the case with internal programming of the motor sequence test. Predictably the SMA would be involved as in Figure 11–2B if a silent counting task was complicated by an internal programming of the movements involved in speaking the numbers. (4) How is the SMA concerned in the production of speech? The answer is that excision of the left SMA by Penfield resulted in aphasia for a period of two weeks, but there was full recovery in time, presumably because of the compensating performance of the right SMA. It would seem that the SMA is concerned with the voluntary initiation of the movements involved in speech, just as with other learned skills. (5) How far is the cerebral cortex to be parceled out into areas of specific function such as areas for voluntary movements, speech, silent counting, and so on? There are now recognized areas related to rhythm and music, to visuomotor activities, and to exploration of extrapersonal space. No doubt, with the elaboration of appropriate psychological tests—for example, for the many varieties of memory and perception—more and more of the cerebral cortex will be assimilated to the patchwork of special functions. A kind of neo-phrenology can be envisaged!

The Freedom of the Will and Moral Responsibility*

It can be appreciated that the demonstration of a free will action is much more convincing when a very simple intention or attention is under consideration than when a human action is studied in some complex physical, social, or moral situation. In the first place it is essential to recognize that most of our actions are learned repertoires of skills, which we carry out automatically without mental concentration or even without conscious awareness, for example, driving a car in light traffic on easy, well-known roads. Mental attention and decision are used only in an emergency. Second, philosophers tend to speculate on freedom of action in some complex social or moral context. For example, if we meet a visiting professor in the street, should we invite him home for dinner? I would not contest the conjecture that such a decision could be freely made, but the difference between this complex situation and that of the finger flexion has an analogy with the attempt to discover the laws of motion by analyzing the eddying movements of a turbulent river instead of the Galilean method with metal balls rolling down an inclined plane!

If we can establish that we have freedom to bring about simple movements at will, then more complex social and moral situations must also in part at least be open to control by a voluntary decision, that is, of mental thought processes. Thus we have opened the way to the consideration of personal freedom and of moral responsibility.

Though theoretically we may be free to choose between alternative responses to a situation, this choice may be vitiated by constraints. In a totalitarian state these constraints are enforced by severe penalties. How far, then, can these unfortunate citizens be held morally responsible for their decisions and actions? Only the brave dare to challenge the power of the state by dissent and to suffer the inhuman consequences. We may ask: How far can the people be held morally responsible for actions done under such constraints? At least we can realize that human freedom is vitiated by constraints applied

*See also Chapter 5.

by a police state. Yet freedom is also corroded in a society that is too permissive of violence and crime.

Considerations of Freedom and Moral Responsibility

The freedom that matters is the freedom to know—freedom of thought, of opinion, of discussion. Such a freedom does not limit the freedom of others, and there can be no doubt that it is fundamental, but as well as ''freedom to know'' we also want freedom in the sphere of action. Freedom to make by our own efforts the utmost out of our lives, to develop ourselves as persons, to give our talents full scope, to live according to our ideals, to control our destiny. This is the freedom that Maritain aptly calls ''freedom in fulfillment.'' This freedom too does not limit the freedom of others. Moreover, the freedom of fulfillment obviously includes the ''freedom to know.'' We can recognize that fullfillment means a full life in the family and in society with loved ones and friends associated in organizations for culture and worship and also for work and recreation. It is the open society of Popper.

How can we set about building our society so that we not only preserve the freedoms we already have but add to them so as to give the fullest possible life to all persons, so creating an order in which all the varying richness of the human personality will be manifested? That should be the central political problem of this age. It is not sufficient, however, to provide such opportunities. Each person should, by his own will, strive to make the most of these opportunities. Freedom involves not only rights but also duties. We have no unqualified right to freedom. We are entitled to freedom only insofar as we fulfill the duties of respecting and living up to the freedom we already have. For example, freedom of fulfillment necessitates a progressive conquest of the fullness of personal life and spiritual liberty. Thus it is evident that we can never attain a static state of freedom. Freedom is dynamic in the sense that we have to be continually striving for it in order even to maintain what we have. Abuse of our freedom endangers it. For example, we endanger our freedom of speech when we use it to make misleading, irresponsible, and provocative statements. The right to freedom of speech presupposes the duty of honesty and sincerity.

Our world is at the parting of the ways. There are only two alternative orders toward which we can move.

One way leads to the centralized planning of the absolutist slave state. In the past a private and personal sphere of life was often able to survive almost untouched by an absolutist tyranny, for despotism was largely devoted to public affairs. With modern efficiency of communication and organization, that is no longer possible. Absolutist governments can stabilize themselves only if they eliminate all resistance before it can organize. Secret police, concentration camps, treason trials, and mass propaganda are the inevitable concomitants. Modern absolutism must be total, enslaving man even in his personal and private life. It must be a tyranny characterized by compulsion, terror, and collectivization of every aspect of life. Such slave states may be very stable.

The other way leads by continuous development to the order of freedom and moral responsibility of each human person. It will be an order respecting and nurturing the private lives of all persons and dependent dynamically on the responsible and free acts of each one of them. At all levels of this open society there will be full play for responsible action. In other words, one of the first considerations will be the widest possible extension of personal responsibility. It is the freely exercised moral choice which most fully expresses personhood and best deserves the great name of freedom.

Conclusions

In conclusion we can say that it is of transcendent importance to recognize that by taking thought we can influence the operation of the neural mechanisms of the brain. In that way we can bring about changes in the world for good or for ill. A simple metaphor is that our conscious self is in the driver's seat. Our whole life can be regarded as made up of successive patterns of choices that could lead to the feeling of fulfillment with the attendant happiness that comes to a life centered on meaning and purpose.

Each human person is a unique self with potentialities that give wonderful promise with all their great diversity. The ideal is for each human person to have the maximum freedom to realize its potentialities. This ethic derives from the belief that life has a transcendental meaning and that each life is precious. Together we are, as human persons, engaged in the tremendous adventure of consciously coexperienced existence.

Suggested Readings

ECCLES, J. C. *Facing reality*. Heidelberg: Springer Verlag, 1970, Ch. 8.

ECCLES, J. C. *The understanding of the brain*. New York: McGraw-Hill, 1973, Ch. 4.

ECCLES, J. C. *The human mystery*. Berlin, Heidelberg New York: Springer Verlag Internat., 1979, Ch. 10.

ECCLES, J. C. *The human psyche*. Berlin, Heidelberg, New York: Springer Verlag Internat., 1980, Chs. 4, 10.

GRANIT, R. *The purposive brain*. Cambridge, Mass.: MIT Press, 1977.

KENNY, A. *Action, emotion and will*. London and Henley: Routlege & Kegan Paul, 1963.

LUCAS, J. R. *The freedom of the will*. London: Oxford University Press, 1970.

PENFIELD, W. *The mystery of the mind*. Princeton, N.J.: Princeton University Press, 1975.

PENFIELD, W., and ROBERTS, L. *Speech and brain mechanisms*. Princeton, N.J.: Princeton University Press, 1959.

POPPER, K. R., ECCLES, J. C. *The self and its brain*. Berlin, Heidelberg, New York: Springer Verlag Internat., 1977, P.2, E3, Dialogue X.

SHERRINGTON, C. S. *Man on his nature*. London: Cambridge University Press, 1940.

12

The Human Adventure: Hope and Death

The Philosophy of Personhood

What we have attempted in this volume is the elucidation and criticism of a number of contemporary views of personhood, particularly those of a materialistic, deterministic bent. It will come as no surprise to the reader that, having found so much wanting and misleading in these views, we arrive at a renewed confidence in the transcendent nature of human life and in its divine origin. But before entering this philosophically perilous realm, we should be quite clear on the connections, such as they are, between the criticisms developed in earlier chapters and an adoption of the religious alternative.

It is a fact of history that most thoroughgoing materialists have regarded materialism as a refutation of religious teaching. Most, *but not all*. In the seventeenth century, for example, the dualism propounded by René Descartes was brilliantly attacked by *Father* Pierre Gassendi, one of the most notable scientists and scholars of his age.

Gassendi knew that an omnipotent God was perfectly able to construct human life according to a totally materialistic scheme and that materialism accordingly could be defended scientifically without colliding with that liberated *Deism* of the seventeenth century. Gassendi is worth mentioning because he offers an especially good example of the compatibility that can exist between deism and materialism. That this compatibility has been rare in history does not mean that it is outlawed in logic. There is no *logical* dilemma created by subscribing simultaneously to the beliefs (1) that all existing entities, including human beings, are totally and exclusively material and (2) that an omnipotent and omniscient Being saw to it that this would be so. An entirely successful materialism would not refute theistic claims, for the latter are addressed not to the material composition of the physical universe but to the *spirit* behind and beyond this universe.

Our opposition to materialism, therefore, has been on exclusively metaphysical and scientific grounds and is not to be read as a veiled *apologia* for religion. With Aristotle, however, we recognize the fact of human intelligence and human intention and accept therefore that intelligence and intention exist. And again with Aristotle we go on to recognize that the evidence we have for *human* intelligence and intention is of *precisely* the same kind as the evidence we would adduce in defense of theism. Aristotle chided the materialists of his own time, noting that "if the art of shipbuilding were in the wood, we would have ships by nature." We do not have ships "by nature" but by design, purpose, skill.

The history of humanity establishes that there are human attributes—moral, intellectual, and aesthetic attributes—that cannot be explained *solely* in terms of the material composition and organization of the brain. Note that we choose the word *cannot*. We *have shown* that all reductionistic attempts fail *in principle* in part through self-refutation and in part through incoherence. This is as true of behavioristic (environmentalistic) and sociobiological (instinctivistic) reductions as of neurophysiological reductions, the promissory materialism treated in Chapters 3 and 4. Actually only the last of these requires attention, for if it fails, the first two necessarily fail. The environment and our genes can be determinative only through the mechanisms and processes of the nervous system. Thus if personhood is not reducible to these mechanisms and processes, neither the behavioristic nor the hereditarian accounts can be sufficient.

Morally we are possessed of "oughts," which, as we have argued, have absolutely no material or physical reference. Intellectually we traffic in *universals,* which are utterly abstract and are not invariably the result of inference, that is, generalizations from past experience. To comprehend that in Riemannian geometry all parallel lines intersect at two loci is not to generalize from past experience, for there has been no such experience, but to fathom the propositional and purely formal character of abstract mathematics. And in filling out our world with the creations of art and architecture, laboring tirelessly for and devotedly revering the "trappings" of civilization (World 3), we show ourselves to be fitted out for more than the life of a creature. The question no longer is one of determining whether and how our brains have made this possible, for in this regard the brain can be no more than the tool and, as such, one step removed from the accomplishments themselves. Leonardo needed many tools (including his brain), but we surely would not seek to explain his genius by studying the knives he used for dissection or the oils he employed in painting. The brain, of course, is not merely one of a number of indifferently useful tools but the *essential* tool and the crowning achievement of evolution—but a tool nonetheless. To say it is a tool for survival and to understand it and its owner only in such terms is to render mindless that actual *life of mind* in which our personhood is rooted. It is instructive again to recall the thoughts of William James in this connection:

> [W]e treat survival as if it were an absolute end, existing as such in the physical world, a sort of actual *should-be,* presiding over the animal and judging his reactions, quite apart from the presence of any commenting intelligence outside. We forget that in the absence of some such superadded commenting intelligence (whether it be that of the animal itself, or only ours or Mr. Darwin's), the reactions cannot be properly talked of as "useful" or "hurtful" at all. Considered merely physically, all that can be said of them is that *if* they occur in a certain way survival will as a matter of fact prove to be their incidental consequence. . . . In a word, survival can enter into a purely physiological discussion only as an *hypothesis made by an onlooker* about the future. But the moment you bring a consciousness into the midst, survival ceases to be a mere hypothesis. No longer is it, "*if* survival is to occur, then so and so must brain and other organs work." It has now become an imperative decree: "Survival *shall* occur, and therefore organs must so work!" *Real* ends appear for the first time now upon the world's stage. [*Principles of Psychology,* Vol. I, p. 141]

We have real ends, though our brains, like our kidneys, do not. There is, then, this separability—though not separation—between the brain and the person who possesses it. And so the question that arises insistently has to do with the fate of the programmer when the computer has ceased to function.

On this, the most consequential of questions, we can rely only on the limited instruments of logic, faith, and common sense. Logic teaches that two mutually contradicting propositions cannot both be true, though the falsity of one does not ensure the truth of the other. But if materialistic determinism is false, is transcendent immaterialism a true account of the person? Aristotle seems to have been of two minds on this, and it is not clear that we have advanced very far beyond his own deep thought. Aware of the human faculty of *epistemonikon*—the faculty by which we are able to comprehend (immaterial, nonspatial, timeless) *universals*—he concluded that the faculty itself could not be material. (What consists of "parts" cannot participate in the realm of universals.) He said of this *epistemonikon* that it does not move (*ou kineitai*), meaning that it lacks the essential attribute of matter, mobility or, more generally, changeability. Being immaterial this same faculty must be indestructable, for only matter undergoes degeneration (change).

This Aristotelian analysis yields very good conceptual grounds on which to defend the soul's survival of the body's (brain's) death. Yet Aristotle followed his own logic to what seemed to be the necessary conclusion; that there cannot be *personal* survival after death. He reasoned thus: For there to be personal survival, there must be the survival of an identifiable individual. But where there is an individual—where there is individuation—there are temporal and spatial boundaries, which is to say there is *matter,* for that which is individuated is *ipso facto* material. The Aristotelian afterlife, then, is more akin to the realm of those Platonic "true forms" than to the heaven promised by Christian scripture. What survives is some sort of rational principle, but surely not a person.

It was (predictably) Thomas Aquinas who found in this analysis a defect, or at least a conceptual element that would be fatal to Christian teaching if correct. Put all too briefly, the Thomistic modification took this form: Every person has knowledge of both particulars and universals. He is the "owner" of both in that his mind contains both and, indeed, compares both. This is all *personal* knowledge possessed by a personally known and knowable mind, e.g. by *my* mind. If, however, no aspect of the universal can make contact of any sort with that which is particular or individual, then it would not be possible for me to recognize that any universal proposition is *my* proposition. This is clearly false, however, and this is sufficient to prove that the individual *soul* is the keeper of *its own* universals. As indicated in Figure 3-1, the soul is individuated not in the material realm but in the realm of spirit (World 2), for the soul is not in the material realm at all. Stating the case in religiously neutral terms, we might say that the rational faculty remains *someone's* faculty in just the sense that every idea is *someone's* idea. It is no more material for being "owned."

What we can say to this point, on these broad Aristotelian and Thomistic grounds, is that there is no compelling reason to accept reductive materialism, and there are several compelling reasons to accept *immaterialism* and the survival of the personal mind-soul following the death of the body. This, however, is as far as metaphysical reasoning will take us, and it is at this point that we must surrender without embarrassment to common sense and the yearnings of faith. That both of these, even with supports provided by metaphysics, cannot settle the question once and for all time is clear from the fact that rational persons can be found who do not unhesitatingly accept the revealed truths of religion. The medieval philosophers often spoke of reason as "faith refining itself." On this noble mission the devout skeptic provides essential services. He obliges us to refine our faith to the utmost, even though we know that in the last analysis it will retain the quality of faith and will not be reason by another name.

Between these poles—the pole of unquestioning faith and that of logicometaphysical rigor—is the wide realm of common sense, the realm we occupy as philophers talk. We fortify our common sense with the study of history, of art and letters, of science, of government and law. We see all around us and throughout history the most extraordinary feats of genius and goodness, its sometimes unacknowledged twin. At every level of social organization and culture we discover persons imbued with a religious sense of life's meaning and deep convictions regarding the awesome mystery that is the human adventure. We read the teachings of the world's prophets and find astonishing similarities among those who could not have known of each other and could not have been formed by similar influences. At the level of common sense we must wonder just why and how these timeless rituals and beliefs came to dominate the human imagination and lead it to notions of transcendence, sublimity, the divine. We reject Darwinian, Freudian, and Marxist explanations, for these as we have seen do not explain *any* notion, let alone ideas of transcendence. We reject materialism because, as we have seen, it doesn't *explain* our concepts but denies them. It is at this point that we, as noble and rational beings, can give vent to the urgings of faith; not faith as the veil of ignorance, sloth, or fear, but faith as a state of mind vindicated by the efforts of reason and common sense.

The Fading of Personhood

We go through life bravely achieving, and so far in this book we have been concentrating on the positive performance that is open to us in the adventure of human personhood. But we all realize that this adventure leads on to the progressive handicaps of aging. So long as we have the full enjoyment of our intellect we can accept our physical deterioration with equanimity. This sets in early for fast responses as in sprinting and jumping and in fast games such as tennis or football, where the summit is attained at about twenty-five years, though it may be somewhat prolonged by high skills. For long-distance running and games of endurance the summit comes later—thirty to thirty-five, and for the Marathon even up to forty. This physical deterioration is attributable to aging of the heart and circulation and respiration as well as of muscle, by biological processes beyond our present understanding. With intellectual performance the summits come later. It is generally believed that in mathematics and poetry the summit is as early as twenty-five to forty. But in science, particularly in the biological sciences, high performance can continue up to sixty and even beyond, while philosophical and artistic creativity may continue well beyond sixty. Thus in Figure 3–4 the arrow of time can extend the cultural performance, and that ineffable quality of wisdom is generally recognized as one of the adornments of the aged, who may be blessed with rich memories and experiences and in whom, surprisingly, illumination by the great gift of imagination may continue as in youth. All these intellectual abilities can be preserved from rapid deterioration by incessant use.

However, we all know that this is but a ''rearguard'' action against the inevitable decline of the brain in aging. The aging process is still a scientific enigma, running a course that may be slower if we are fortunate in our genetic inheritance and in our freedom from diseases that specifically cause brain damage, which is particularly tragic in the greatly accelerated aging of Alzheimer's Syndrome. We are apt to envy those who after a full life die in a sudden episode of heart or brain. They escape from the progressive deterioration that is our particular concern, with our overriding themes of hope and meaning in the adventure of personhood. We can ask, How can the adventure of personhood be reconciled with mental deterioration? In Figure 3–4 this would be diagrammed by a diminution of the boxes of World 2 and World 3 when followed further upward with the arrow of time. Yet we can have acceptance of this progressive decline of memories if the cherished memories remain, as they do if encouraged by recall. This is the age when refuge may be taken in autobiography or in reminiscing often to the boredom of our friends! Certainly we do not welcome growing old in solitude. With loved ones aging together there can be a mutual source of joy. More often these days the distractions of TV keep away all thoughts and fears of aging personhood. At any rate, in a fully lived personhood there should be integration of our aging.

So far we have considered two extremes, the sudden death or the slow deterioration with no cerebral accidents on the way. But often there can be severe brain lesions with survival even for decades. Great courage is often shown by these victims and their helpmeets. In fact, we all need courage in the last years of our life. But more important is the great gift of love that can be shared right to the end. Ideally the adventure of human personhood begins with the baby and child in the loving environment of the family and ends in a loving atmosphere that can continue on to the end in death.

The famous author Freya Stark wrote most movingly on aging, death and the hope of a life hereafter:

> Our private grasp lessens, and leaves us heir to infinite loves in a common world where every joy is a part of one's personal joy. With a loosening hold returning towards acceptance, we prepare in the anteroom for a darkness where even this last personal flicker fades, and what happens will be in the Giver's hand alone.

It is a great contrast from this humility to the arrogant farewell of the English poet Walter Savage Landor:

> I strove with none, for none was worth my strife,
> Nature I loved and, next to Nature, Art:
> I warmed both hands before the fire of life;
> It sinks, and I am ready to depart.

Death and Immortality?

On all materialist theories of the mind there can be no consciousness of any kind after brain death. Immortality is a nonproblem. But with dualist-interactionism it can be recognized from the standard diagram (Figure 3-1) that death of the brain need not result in the destruction of the central component of World 2. All that can be inferred is that World 2 (the programmer) ceases to have any relationship with the brain (the computer) and hence will lack all sensory information and all motor expression from and to this material world, including the brains of living persons. There is no question of a continued shadowy or ghostlike existence in some relationship with the material world, as claimed in some spiritualist beliefs. What then can we say?

Belief in some life after death came very early to mankind, as is indicated by the ceremonial burial customs of Neanderthal man. In our earliest records of beliefs about life after death, however, it was most unpleasant. This can be seen in the Epic of Gilgamesh, in the Homeric poems, or in the Hebrew belief about Sheol. Hick points out that the misery and unhappiness believed to attend the life hereafter very effectively disposes of the explanation that such beliefs arose from wish fulfillment!

The idea of a more attractive afterlife is a special feature of the Socratic dialogues, being derived from the Orphic mysteries. There was a particularly clear affirmation of immortality by Socrates in the *Phaedo* just before his death:

> If the soul is immortal, it demands our care not only for that part of the time which we call life, but for all time; . . . since the soul is clearly immortal, it can have no escape or security from evil except by becoming as good and wise as it possibly can. For it takes nothing with it to the next world except its education and training.
>
> . . . Said Crito: "But how shall we bury you?" "Any way you like," replied Socrates, "that is if you can catch me and I don't slip through your fingers." He laughed gently as he spoke, and turning to us went on: "I can't persuade Crito that I am Socrates here who is talking to you now and marshalling all the arguments; he thinks that I am the one whom he will see presently lying dead; and he asks how he is to bury me! As for my long and elaborate explanation that when I have drunk the poison I shall remain with you no longer, but depart to a state of heavenly happiness, this attempt to console both you and myself seems to be wasted on him."

After the poignant simplicity of Socrates' messages before death, it is quite an experience to contemplate the many kinds of immortality that have been the subject of speculation. The idea of immortality has been sullied over and even made repugnant by the many attempts from the earliest religions to give an account that was based on the ideologies of the time. Thus today intellectuals are put off by these archaic attempts to describe and depict life after bodily death. We are put off by them too. It is not valuable to speculate on this "body"–soul problem after death. It is perplexing enough during life! Self-recognition and communication may be possible for the psyche in ways beyond our imagination.

We normally have the body and brain to assure us of our identity, but, with departure of the psyche from the body and brain in death, none of these landmarks is available to it. All of the detailed memory must be lost. If we refer again to Figure 3–1, memory is also shown located in World 2. Perhaps this is a more general memory related to our self-identity, our emotional life, our personal life, and our ideals as enshrined in the values—in fact the whole identity of the programmer. All of this should be sufficient for self-identity. Reference should be made to the discussion on the creation of the psyche by infusion into the developing embryo. *This divinely created psyche should be central to all considerations of immortality and of self-recognition* as suggested by H. D. Lewis. With the disintegration of our computer with brain death, we have lost this wonderful instrument, the most intimate companion of a lifetime. Is there no further existence for the programmer?

It was this question that had obsessed Gustav Mahler and formed the theme of his great Symphony No 2, in C minor, that is called appropriately the "Resurrection." The choral conclusion of the last movement (the Fifth) leads up finally to the climax for which Mahler wrote actually the following words given in German with an English translation:*

ALTO
O glaube, mein Herz, or glaube,
es geht dir nichts verloren!
Dein ist, was du gesehnt,
dein was du geliebt,
was du gestritten!

O glaube,
du warst nicht umsonst geboren!
Has nicht umsonst gelebt,
gelitten!

CHORUS
Was entstanden ist,
das muss vergehen!
Was vergangen, aufersteh'n!

ALTO
O believe, my heart, o believe,
naught will be lost to you!
What you longed for is yours,
yours what you loved,
what you championed!

O believe,
you were not born in vain!
You have not lived in vain
nor suffered!

CHORUS
What was created
must pass away!
What passed away must rise!

* English translation by William Mann ©; with acknowledgments.

Hör auf zu beben!	*Cease to tremble!*
Bereite dich zu leben!	*Prepare yourself to live!*

SOPRANO AND ALTO	SOPRANO AND ALTO
O Schmerz! Du Alldurchdringer,	*O suffering! You that pierce all things,*
dir bin ich entrungen!	*from you I am wrested away!*
O Tod! Du Allbezwinger,	*O death! you that overcome all things,*
nun bist du bezwungen!	*now you are overcome!*
Mit Flügeln, die ich mir errungen,	*With wings that I wrested for myself*
in beissem Liebesstreben,	*in the fervent struggle of love*
werd' ich entschweben	*I shall fly away*
zum Licht, zu dem kein Aug' gedrungen!	*to the light wither no eye pierced.*

CHORUS	CHORUS
Sterben werd' ich, um zu leben!	*Die I shall, so as to live!*

TUTTI	TUTTI
Aufersteh'n wirst du,	*Rise again you will,*
mein Herz, in einem NU!	*my heart, in a trice!*
Was du geschlagen,	*What you have conquered*
zu Gott wird es dich tragen!	*will carry you to God!*

The Quest for Meaning

Our life here on this earth and in this cosmos is beyond our understanding in respect of the great questions. We have to be open to some deep dramatic significance in this earthly life of ours that may be revealed after the transformation of death. We can ask: What does this life mean? We find ourselves here in this wonderfully rich and vivid conscious experience, and it goes on through life. But is that the end? This self-conscious mind of ours has this mysterious relationship with the brain, and as a consequence achieves experiences of human love and friendship, of the wonderful natural beauties, and of the intellectual excitement and joy given by appreciation and understanding of our cultural heritages. Is this present life all to finish in death, or can we have hope that there will be further meaning to be discovered? In the context of natural theology we can say only that there is complete oblivion about the future—but we came from oblivion. Is it that this life of ours is simply an episode of consciousness between two oblivions, or is there some further transcendent experience of which we can know nothing until it comes?

Man has lost his way ideologically in this age. It is what has been called the predicament of mankind. How often are we immersed in evil happenings in the world as recounted in the media? This evil is perpetrated by states, by terrorist gangs and organizations, or by individuals. The inherent decency and goodness of human persons goes almost unproclaimed in the overwhelming cacophony—hence our predicament. Our ideological confusion presents a tremendous challenge for all idealists, creative writers, and thinkers to recognize and confront these evils with their opposites: the oppression of tyrannical states with the freedom of the open society; lies and deceit with truth; fanaticism with reason; terrorism with peace; the arrogance of power seekers with humility; the cult of ugliness with beauty.

We think science has gone too far in breaking down man's belief in his spiritual greatness, as exemplified in the magnificent achievements in World 3, and has given him the belief that he is merely an insignificant animal that has arisen by chance and necessity in an insignificant planet lost in the great cosmic immensity. This is the message given to us by Monod in *Chance and Necessity*. The principal trouble with mankind today is that the intellectual leaders are too arrogant in their self-sufficiency. We must realize the great unknowns in the material makeup and operation of our brains, in the relationship of brain to mind, in our creative imagination, and in the uniqueness of the psyche. *When we think of these unknowns as well as the unknown of how we come to be in the first place, we should be much more humble.*

We can have hope as we recognize and appreciate the wonder and mystery of our existence as experiencing selves. Mankind would be cured of its alienation if that message could be expressed with all the authority of scientists and philosophers as well as with the imaginative insights of artists. In this book we express our efforts to understand a human person, namely ourself, as an experiencing being. We offer it in the hope that it may help man to discover a way out of his alienation and to face up to the terrible and wonderful reality of his existence—with courage and faith and hope. We pray that man may develop a transforming faith in the meaning and significance of this wonderful, even unbelievable, adventure given to each of us on this lovely and salubrious earth of ours, itself a mere grain in the infinite cosmos of galaxies. Because of the mystery of our being as unique self-conscious existences, we can have hope as we set our own soft, sensitive, and fleeting personal experience against the terror and immensity of illimitable space and time. Are we not participants in the meaning, where there is else no meaning? Do we not experience and delight in fellowship, joy, harmony, truth, love, and beauty, where otherwise there is only the mindless universe?

We have the strong belief that we have to be open to the future in the adventure of human personhood. This whole cosmos is not just running on and running down for no meaning. In the context of natural theology we come to the belief that we are creatures with some supernatural meaning that is as yet ill defined. We cannot think more than that we are all part of some great design. Each of us can have the belief of acting in some unimaginable supernatural drama. We should give all we can in order to play our part in this life on earth. Then we wait with serenity and joy for the future revelations of whatever is in store after bodily death.

Suggested Readings

BADHAM, P. *Christian beliefs about life after death,* London: SPCK, 1976.

DOBZHANSKY, T. *The biology of ultimate concern.* New York: New American Library, 1967.

ECCLES, J. C. *Facing reality.* Heidelberg: Springer Verlag, 1970, Chs. 10, 12.

ECCLES, J. C. *The human psyche.* Berlin, Heidelberg, New York: Springer Verlag Internat., 1980, Ch.10.

HEISENBERG, W. *Physics and beyond, encounters and conversations.* London: George Allen and Unwin, 1971.

LEWIS, H. D. *Persons and life after death.* London: Macmillan, 1978.

PEACOCKE, A. R. *Science and the Christian experiment.* London: Oxford University Press, 1971.

PENFIELD, W. *The mystery of the mind.* Princeton, N. J.: Princeton University Press, 1975.

PLANCK, M. *Scientific autobiography and other papers.* London: Williams and Norgate, 1950.

POPPER, K. R., and ECCLES, J. C. *The self and its brain.* Berlin, Heidelberg, New York: Springer Verlag Internat., 1977, Dialogues III, XI.

SHERRINGTON, C. S. *Man on his nature.* London: Cambridge University Press, 1940.

THORPE, W. H. *Biology, psychology and belief.* London: Cambridge University Press, 1961.

THORPE, W. H. *Animal nature and human nature.* London: Methuen, 1974.

THORPE, W. H. *Purpose in a world of chance: A biologist's view.* Oxford: Oxford University Press, 1978.

Index